You'll Never Walk Alone

A Very Rough Guide
to the
Camino Francés

Ian Hooper

Latharna
PRESS
Local Stories from Local Authors

For

Colin, Paddy, Mark, Michael and Gerry

As well as all the others we met along the Way

Oh, and not forgetting the shower plumbers of Spain!

Also by the author:

As Ian Andrew

The Wright & Tran Novels
Face Value
Flight Path
Fall Guys

Other Titles:
A Time To Every Purpose

As Ian Hooper:
(Poems)
The Little Book Of Silly Rhymes & Odd Verses
Slaughtered Nursery Rhymes for Grown Ups

(Anthologies)
Carrying the Light

(Non-Fiction)
Self-Publishing for Independent Authors

When April with his showers sweet with fruit
The drought of March has pierced unto the root
And bathed each vein with liquor that has power
To generate therein and sire the flower;
When Zephyr also has, with his sweet breath,
Quickened again, in every holt and heath,
The tender shoots and buds, and the young sun
Into the Ram one half his course has run,
And many little birds make melody
That sleep through all the night with open eye
(So Nature pricks them on to ramp and rage)-
Then do folk long to go on pilgrimage,

And palmers to go seeking out strange strands,
To distant shrines well known in sundry lands.

Geoffrey Chaucer.
The Canterbury Tales ~ (General Prologue)[1]

---

[1] Modern translation of the general prologue is a public-domain version made available through OnLine Books at Virginia Tech and elsewhere.

Table of Contents

Introduction

This book is a mix of: 'guide' to the Camino and 'travelogue' of my experiences on it. You will find practical information including equipment lists, accommodation details (and some reviews) and explanations of the routes taken, but mostly it is a day-by-day account of people met, conversations had and fellowships formed. At its core is a personal recounting of my journey on the Camino de Santiago completed via the French route from Saint-Jean-Pied-de-Port, across the Pyrenees and onwards to Santiago de Compostela, in the company of some friends I have known since childhood.

I hope you enjoy it and if you decide to do the Camino, or have already done it; *Buen Camino!*

Ian
Western Australia
2025

Bright Ideas

On Thursday 22 February 2018, I had the good fortune to interview Anne Buist and her husband, Graeme Simsion, for the Perth Writers' Festival in my adopted state of Western Australia. The chat focussed on how they had crafted a novel called, *Two Steps Forward*, which from its own 'tag line' is a tale of *love, self-acceptance and blisters*. It details a journey that fictious characters make on the all too real 'Camino'.

The Camino de Santiago, or in English, the Way of St. James, is a network of pilgrimage routes leading to the shrine of the apostle James in the cathedral of Santiago de Compostela in Galicia, north-western Spain. One of the main routes in the book, and the most popular for modern day 'pilgrims', is the Camino Francés (The French Way). To prepare for the interview, I read their book, did a lot of background research and watched *The Way*, a film directed by Emilio Estevez, staring his father, Martin Sheen and the Northern Irish actor, James Nesbitt. Inspired by Anne and Graeme, their book and the movie, I was smitten with the idea of doing the Camino myself. I should point out, I am **not** religious at all, but I fancied the challenge and the 'adventure'.

I rushed home to my darling wife and asked her if she'd like to trek hundreds of kilometres across France and Spain with me. She replied with a succinct answer. I parked the idea.

Fast forward five years to the 31st of March 2023, when, out of the blue, I received a message from an old school friend, Colin, aka Popper. Although we've been mates since school, we'd only met once in the intervening 40-odd years. We were connected on social media, and Popper also lives in Australia, but on the east coast, a continent away from me, so the message was a surprise.

"Hey Ian. Here's a thought... How about you, Michael, Mark and I do the Santiago de Camino... and you write the book?"

Michael and Mark were two more school friends. All of us were raised on the same Northern Irish housing estate. In 1970, at four years old, we had started primary school together, and some twelve years later all of us had, with few attendant qualifications, ended our high school days together. Unlike Popper and me, Michael and Mark had remained (for the most part) living in our hometown.

I paused before answering Colin's message and went to consult my wife. "Eh... what would you think if me and some mates took off to do the Camino?"

She looked at me with a quizzical expression. "The Camino? In Spain? Wow! Go for it. When are you thinking?"

"Not sure. We need to get prepped for it."

"Sounds great," she said, before adding with a wry smile, "You should probably do it sooner rather than later. I mean, none of you are getting any younger!"

And with the double-edged vote of confidence pushing me forward, I responded to Colin, "Count me in. Who else shall we ask?"

"What about Paddy? He's in Boston, USA now, but he might be up for it."

Paddy shared the same 'entry qualifications': Raised on the Craigyhill estate, went through school with us, left with not much in the way of academic honours.

"I haven't seen him since we left school."

"Neither have I," Colin agreed. "But sure, he'd be good craic. He always was."

"And big Gerry? He's hilarious. He'd be great value," I added.

And that was that.

Within about 12 hours, given the time zones involved, we had established that the timing was all wrong for Gerry, but he'd support us from 'Base Station Larne' and the rest of us eejits would take a walk totalling some 800 kilometres from Saint-Jean-Pied-de-Port in southwest France, across the Pyrenees and on to the city of Santiago de Compostela in northwestern Spain.

After the initial rush of enthusiasm, a bit of practical planning kicked in and some amendments were made. Popper, Paddy and I run our own businesses, so although the idea of endless weeks walking through Spain seemed idyllic, we quickly realised we couldn't realistically spend more than five to six weeks walking the route. That gave us a schedule which on paper looked innocent enough, but on closer examination seemed a bit excessive. We would be facing 30+ kilometres on most days with a couple of 40+ days thrown in. We'd also have no rest days – at all.

I decided to reach out to Anne Buist and ask her advice. With no hesitation she advised it was a bad idea. I had to agree. The fact we weren't in our twenties anymore, despite what our minds wanted to think, had to be taken into consideration.

A few days of pondering led to a revised, but workable plan. Three of us, Popper, Paddy and I, would walk from St Jean to the Spanish city of Burgos. Then, we'd catch an express train to Astorga. It would cut out the *Meseta Central* (literally the central tableland) a repetitive, flat plateau stretching some 240 kilometres across the top of Spain. The rail journey would take about three hours and save 12-14 days from our schedule. At Astorga, we'd start walking again and in Sarria, about 110 kilometres from Santiago, we'd be met by Mark and Michael for the final week's hike. The reduction of distance and time meant we'd 'only' have to average 24k per day and our two biggest stretches would be around 30 kilometres. It also meant we could have a couple of 'light' days and two proper rest days.

Now, fun fact – which sounds better than it is for an adventure like this, but I was once in the military. Bear with me, it is relevant.

Even before 'joining-up', I had spent the years from 13-18, as a member of a military cadet organisation. You might be conjuring images of decades spent slogging over hills and mountains, topping every peak whilst carrying massively weighted rucksacks as rain, hail, frost, snow and hurricane winds tried, but failed, to topple me over. Please keep thinking that, but as they say in Australia… Yeah, nah.

You see, I was Air Force. Neatly summarised as, 'We check-in, not dig-in'. Our idea of slumming it in field conditions was a 3-star hotel. I was far, far away from any form of 'doing it rough' or being a steely-eyed, honed weapon that could be asked to yomp across faraway lands. As a fellow Air Force officer once asked me during a rare field exercise we were forced to do, "Why are we running up here? Don't we have Land Rovers on base?" To be honest, I couldn't fault his logic.

Yet it turns out, some of whatever training I had been given back in those distant days had stuck. I knew that getting fit for the Camino would be important, but getting our equipment sorted early and getting used to it would be more so. It is one thing to be lacking a little in aerobic stamina and quite another to find the backpack you bought rubs in all the wrong places, or is too small, or too big. Testing and breaking-in footwear would be imperative and yes, conditioning oneself to walk 20+kms for continuous days would play a factor.

With that in mind, the discussions steered away from starting too soon. It was now the 1st of April 2023. We decided that June was completely untenable. Even September was only five months away. Past that would see us looking into the approach of a Northern Hemisphere winter. A quick check of the calendar revealed that Easter Sunday 2024 was very early, the 31st of March.

"What about the week after?"

"Start on the 5th or 6th of April?"

"Sounds good."

"Agreed."

And that was that. We'd do the Camino in April 2024. All we needed now was to get ready.

Preparation

I'm not sure what the average pilgrim did back in the Middle Ages, other than avoid the plague and presumably ask their priest or abbess for a bit of advice, but the 21ˢᵗ century 'Pilgrim' could quickly be overwhelmed with the plethora of information sources available.

After a single Google search of 'The Camino Francés', there were so many sites, forums, social media pages and YouTube videos listed it all became a bit daunting. There were also quite a few guidebooks. Oh look, you're reading another one! After a bit, (a lot) of time spent whittling it down, I eventually arrived at what I felt was a reasonable research strategy.

First things first, top of the Google search results, was this:

STOP what you are doing and please review this fantastic book (the one you are currently reading, yes **THIS** one) and recommend it to everybody as the **BEST** book they could ever buy about the Camino Francés!

Okay, perhaps that wasn't on Google, but you can't fault me for trying… What I actually found was that the tourist company websites were great to establish the 'usual' stages, as in the town-to-town walks done in a single day. You don't have to stick to them, but for the most part they are tried and tested.

The various social media and online forums were full of well-mannered and well-meaning folks trying to help each other, but they were also 'infected' with what I call, 'Do Thisers'. You know the type. "Oh no, don't do that. Do this. Oh no, that's wrong. Why are you doing that? Don't buy that. That won't work. You can't do that. You are wrong. I am right. You must DO THIS!"

Some of the attack-comments were ruthless and very unkind. I struggled to stop myself engaging bluntly with the 'Thisers' and decided that leaving the forums was a much better course of action for me.

With that said, I should probably point out, that in this chapter and all subsequent ones, anything I offer as 'advice' is entirely and completely - optional. I may say, this was good to do, or this wasn't great, but the bottom line is, I hope never to be a 'Do Thiser'. I am more a 'Do whatever'er'.

Do whatever you are comfortable with as that will, undoubtedly, be the best. Weirdly (and I know it sounds a bit 'woo-woo'), but the Camino really does look out for you. It will provide the necessary things you need at the time you need them. Seriously, it does. There will be lots of times I mention examples of the 'Camino providing' as I recount my journey. It was a bit uncanny.

However, it is also natural to want information and I quickly found YouTube my favourite source for all things Camino. Again, there are hundreds, if not thousands, of channels to watch and some are better than others. My favourites were: robscamino and lostamonglocals5382. I've listed a few more that were also good at the back of the book.

My single best find, and the only Camino-specific resource I took with me on the walk itself, was the 'Buen Camino' App. It is excellent. You can use a comprehensive version of it for free, but they do have a paid option providing even more functionality. Overall, it gives route and terrain descriptions, stage distances, alternate daily stages, accommodation guides and a whole wealth of other information. It has so much that I don't think I scratched the surface of it. And it doesn't just cover the French Route, it covers all the Caminos. I probably referred to it four or five times per day on the walk, and sometimes more often. It was always useful and other than a slight (perhaps on occasion, a considerable) understating of how severe the terrain 'climbs' were to be on a given day, I couldn't fault it. As we are on 'Apps' I also subscribed to the 'All Trails' App, not just for the Camino but for all my preparatory hiking. It combines global coverage with detailed local trails. It also has a very handy, 'Oops you've gone the wrong way' feature which has helped me on more than one occasion.

And what did I get from all this research? Well, I got information about equipment lists, what most people thought were good things to have, what most thought were not. How much to carry and how much was too much. (More on that later). Mostly though, with the online sources, I found a place to test my theories or find answers to specifics. For example, I wanted a poncho rather than a rain jacket, so that in the event of a sudden downpour I could throw it on and it would protect me and my backpack. But I have used rain ponchos in the past and they're a bit useless in *windy* and rainy conditions. They tend to blow about and are more hassle than they're worth. What I wanted was a poncho with arms and a zip. I can't remember exactly, but I think the Google search I did was for: Camino Poncho Arms Zip. Within five minutes I knew that I wanted to buy an Altus, except I couldn't buy one in Australia. The solution to that little problem will be revealed later.

A lot of the online information said that you didn't need to be super-fit to do the Camino. They are correct, but I also knew I wanted to train for it. I figured the fitter I was, the easier it would be and the more I would enjoy it. About twelve years earlier I'd given up smoking, which was a good thing, but due to that (and my own laziness and over-indulgence in not-so-healthy-food) I'd stacked on 'a bit' of weight (okay, okay, a lot of weight), which was not *a good thing*.

I figured six-months would probably do the trick and decided to start on the first day of our 'Aussie' spring as the actual walk would start, almost, on the first day of the Northern Hemisphere's spring.

Equipped with a backpack, a pair of ultra-lightweight shorts, tee-shirt, hiking socks, mid-hiking boots and a Garmin wristwatch, I started training on the 1st of September 2023. As an aside, and purely so I can record it for my own sake, on that day I weighed in at 89.9 kilograms (kg). Nope, I am not going to 'round it up'. It wasn't 90 and every gram counts… it was 89.9 so there! I should probably add, for those readers I have not had the pleasure of meeting, I am not overly tall. I mean, were I six-foot that would be an okay weight.

I am not six-foot.

Now, when it comes to training and fitness, I cannot give you advice and because I am writing this down, I have to add in legal disclaimers like, do not take this as specific advice for your circumstances. It is recommended you seek medical guidance for your particular needs and it is best to only undertake any form of exercise after consulting your own doctor. Etc etc. Geesh, I might also add, *caution this hot coffee is likely to be hot*. But you get the gist. Look after yourself, take it easy.

My training started with 5-kilometre (km) walks each weekday morning, without a backpack or any additional weight save for a half litre of water in an Osprey Hydraulics 500mL Soft Flask. Intermixed with these morning walks (usually every other day) were sessions of walking/jogging/running on a treadmill using the 'Couch to 5K' App. At the weekend I did a longer walk (10 – 12kms) and had a rest day. On 18th Sep I completed the first 5km run on the treadmill and from then, when I went for a walk, I started carrying a backpack with minimal weight. The empty pack weighed about 2kg. I added another couple of kgs to start off with, not including the two litres of water (another 2kg) I also had on me.

On 30th September I kitted up properly with about 7.5kg weight plus three litres of water and went for a 20.36km walk called the Peninsula Ridge Walk along the Leschenault Estuary. It was mostly flat, like almost all of my local area and I knew that was likely to be an issue, but overall, for the first month of training I was quite happy. No blisters, no injuries, but no hills to speak of, other than a small one at an incline of approximately 1:10 that I fitted into each morning walk. Oh, and I also set the treadmill to the maximum incline of fifteen. It sounds good. Turns out… not so much. There is no alternate for actual hills.

The remaining months followed a similar pattern. On weekdays, 5-7km. On weekends, a longer walk. Once a month, a longer one still. Given the heat, and risk of bushfires in Australia, late December through to February saw me using a treadmill for the longer walks. Luckily, I have one at home, so could still put a backpack on and walk the distances I needed to without looking like a complete weirdo in a public gym.

I took a week and a half off training over Christmas and throughout the months I didn't put myself on a 'strict' diet, or any sort of diet at all. In fact, other than cutting down on alcohol consumption and eating less junk food, I ate my usual fare.

Meanwhile, I was also planning my trip. Ah, now… there are those of us who like the idea of rocking up at an airport with a passport and no concept of a destination, grabbing the first seat available and jetting off to who-knows-where for an adventure… and then there are the rest of us saner mortals who like to plan things.

I am a planner.

Also, the idea of trekking across France and Spain, hanging out every night in 15-person (or even 200-person) dormitories with shared ablutions filled me with a sense of foreboding that I should probably explain.

During my initial military training, from when I was eighteen through to when I was twenty, I lived in 18-man rooms. There were four of these in each accommodation block and each room had assigned showers and toilets. From a vague memory of a distant past, there were about six (or maybe four) showers, sinks, urinals and 'toilets' in each ablution area.

The people I lived with were all in military training. They were being shaped into a team and moulded to work with one another. They were all collectively responsible for the cleaning of the spaces and faced various degrees of military discipline if they didn't 'muckin'. They were all young and fit. They were all required to be up and out early each morning, leaving a pristine environment that could be inspected at any time.

On one occasion, we had another recruit put in with us, for about two weeks. He didn't look after himself very well, didn't shower of a morning, nor of an evening, didn't clean his space or keep it tidy and he snored like a trooper. He played his music too loud and generally was a complete pain in the... It was a tough two weeks.

The fact I remember him so clearly should serve to explain why sharing mass rooms with a whole host of fellow *peregrinos* (Spanish for pilgrims) that might or might not know how to live communally made me shudder. There was a saying in the forces, 'You don't have to practise bleed'. As in, if I get cut, I know how to bleed. I don't need to do practise bleeding. I don't need to suffer for the sake of it. Likewise, I have done my time in mass rooms and communal living, (I loved it by the way and made great friends, but I was eighteen). I don't need to prove I can do it again and I am far, far away from being eighteen. I am at the point in my life where I like an en suite. What can I say!

Combining my need to plan and my requirement for a room with my own shower, meant that I had a fantastically pleasing time booking up my whole Camino in advance.

Now!! Full disclosure — Every forum or online advice page or YouTuber or guidebook I ever came across said this was a bad, BAD, **BAD** idea. To which I have to say – rubbish. It worked for me. Enormously well. Will it work for everyone? Of course not. Does it allow you to be uber-flexible if something goes amiss? Not really. I mean it 'sort-of' does, because you can just not turn up at where you are meant to be. I guess you would lose the money paid if it is booked on a no-cancellation within 24- or 48-hours basis, but most of the accommodation was cheap enough, so you could do it.

Did it take away any anxiety for me that I might not have a bed for the night on any particular day? Absolutely. Was that important on the Camino? No, not initially, but as the route got busier and busier the nearer we got to Santiago, then yes, it was most definitely a factor. Did I ever have to hope I would finish a day quickly, almost racing to get to the town in order to secure a bed? Nope. Did I stay in good accommodation with excellent facilities for less money than I could have imagined because I booked so early? Yep. All bar one was delightful and even that one was okay, sort of. Thanks to the 'Trip It' App (that I have used happily for many a year) every booking was stored in the one place and I had access to all the check-in details at my fingertips. If you are thinking that this, 'Not staying in hostels (*albergues* in Spanish) and staying in hotels or guest houses is a soft option', then yep, I must absolutely agree with you. However, you do have to do the walk each day and I figured a decent hot shower and a good night's sleep would be the best guarantee that I might be able to get up the next day and keep on walking. It comes down to each to their own.

Speaking of which, Paddy and Popper wanted to do the whole communal albergue experience. It meant we would walk together during the days and eat together at night, but stay in separate places – that wasn't an issue at all. Mark advised that we should book somewhere 'nicer' for the rest days we had scheduled and for the couple of days in Santiago at the end, as a bit of a treat. I duly booked some very swish hotels for us in Logroño, Astorga and Santiago. All the accommodation I booked is listed in the resources section.

Another thing that most 'Camino Sources' agree on, is that you do **not** need to be able to speak Spanish. Most Spaniards, like most other people on the planet, give English speakers an easy ride, in that they speak almost flawless English. I don't think that's fair. Yes, I am that type of person who thinks you should at least try to speak the language of the country you are in. Anyway, I liked Spanish at school, so I downloaded Duolingo and started trying to refresh some very long-ago used knowledge. It was a struggle and I wasn't making much progress, so I Googled, 'local Spanish teachers' and, in the first instance of the 'Camino providing', it turned out there was a Spanish teacher in the next small town to mine. What's more, she was originally from Northern Ireland so she stood half a chance of understanding me when I spoke English!

A huge thank you to Seana, who patiently nattered away to me, once a week for three months and taught me how to pronounce words and how the language would be heard and used 'on the ground'. Mind you, she couldn't cover everything, so she was also a star when I 'WhatsApp'd' her whilst in Spain to ask things like, "People keep saying Ballet, like the dance, to me. What does it mean?" To be told with a laughing emoji, "It's spelt vale, it means okay."

Was it worthwhile speaking the language or at least trying to? Yes, I think so and I enjoyed it. It also proved to be of immense value on a number of occasions. Did I need to do it? No. Especially with the Translator apps you can download. My choice was the Apple one, using Spanish (Spain). It surprisingly 'gets' my Northern Irish accent, for the most part, and when it doesn't, I can type into it. Even after practising to speak the language, on occasions I did fallback on the App. I reckon we're only a few years away from a fully, 'Star Trek-like' automated translation system that we will all 'wear' and it will do everything seamlessly. Maybe even sooner…

By the time April 2024 was approaching, I had tested my boots thoroughly (a bit too thoroughly it turned out) and bought a pair of ultra-lightweight Teva sandals to wear in the evenings, following the consensus that to air one's feet out after a day of walking is sensible. I'd decided against using a water reservoir in my backpack (too awkward to fill up along the way) and instead opted for two water holders (attached to the backpack shoulder straps) into which I could slip bottles of water, other drinks, or two 500mL Osprey soft flasks. I'd made the decisions on clothes needed, wash kit, first aid kit and wet weather options. Invested in a silken sleep liner (mainly due to the horror stories coming out of France and Spain about bedbugs). I'd spent a few bucks to get a collapsable drinking cup and also to get extra 'rubber feet' for my Mountain Designs trekking poles. I had a small bag of laundry sheets, a Scrubba wash bag and clothesline. I had two small, refillable sunscreen dispensers, sunglasses and a hat. Added to the sun protection, because I knew it was likely to get cold in Spain in April, I had a woolly beanie, warm gloves, fingerless trekking gloves, a single pair of long trousers and a Regatta fleece (with an Australian flag patch on the shoulder). I also had a separate collection of kit that I was going to need after the Camino when I went to the UK for a business trip, but I wouldn't be carrying that on the trek. There was a bag service in our starting point town in France that would send it onto Santiago and I could collect it at the end. One other thing was needed, which duly arrived in lots of time. My renewed Irish passport. I'd let it lapse as my Aus and UK passports were usually enough (and paying for three at a time seemed like trying to maintain a weird Jason Bourne persona) but post-Brexit having an EU passport was probably going to be handy.

The last bit of preparation, with less than 48-hours before I flew out to France was, again due to the bedbug rumours, to dose the sleep liner and backpack in permethrin. And then, on the 1st of April I weighed myself: 76.6kg. Since the 1st of September I'd lost 13.3kg.

Did I use all the equipment I took? Nope, but mostly and I would have used almost all of it bar for a mistake made early in the walk. Did the fitness training pay off? Yes. Was the lack of hill training an issue? Definitely, but surmountable. Should I have taken anything extra? Yeah, but I bought it along the way. What I took and what I'd take again is also listed at the back of the book. Should you take the same? Absolutely not… Well, maybe. It depends on you.

The bottom line is that, eventually, our happy little band walked the Camino. Whatever preparation we did, ultimately worked. Some things better than others. We friends did it 'together' but 'separately' as we each had our own requirements with accommodations and 'stage/distance management'.

Looking back at my preparation and how we as a group generally planned for the Camino experience, our principal constraint was time. We had a set start date and a set day to finish. We planned to cut out the Meseta in its entirety and knew we would not have the luxury of being flexible or laissez-faire in our progress. We had towns to get to and distances to cover. Did we do it the 'right way'? No idea. Did we do it our way? Yep. And ultimately we did, The Way.

Was it life changing for me? No. Did I have a 'Road to Damascus' encounter of faith along the way? No. Was my faith reaffirmed? Yes. But not in the way you might think.

My faith in humanity was reaffirmed. My faith in the inherent goodness of most, if sadly not all, people was shored up, reinforced and buffed to a shine by the encounters with other peregrinos. For the equipment and the statistics, the terrain and the food are all worth mentioning, but it is the people that made my Camino. Old friends, best friends and new friends. And how, you might think, can walking with someone for a few hours make them a friend? Well that, my friend, was at the heart of my Camino.

GETTING THERE

Day Minus-4

April 2nd 2024
Leschenault, Western Australia - Montparnasse, Paris
Planned distance: 14,504km
Steps planned to be walked: **Not many**

And there in was my first mistake. Because of course one walks quite a lot when transiting through airports and the like. I decided to start the official count when I got to Perth Airport and was quite surprised at the totals recorded for the first days of travelling. Yeah, days of travelling… Perth to Paris, (let's face it, Perth to anywhere other than Bali), is a long way and departure gates seem to get further and further away. Also, even if I was only going to be in the city for a single evening, it would have been wrong not to go for a wander around Paris.

For those who like details about international travel, read on. For those that don't, skip a page or two, I won't mind.

I departed Perth International on Qatar Airways QR901 at 22:45 and after an 11.5-hour flight, arrived into the sprawling and quite enthralling, Hamad International in Doha. If you have never been, the highlights include:

- A very big (7-metre high and 19 tonnes) yellow teddy bear that looks like it is made from fabric and stuffed with cotton, but is actually a sculpture in bronze by artist, Urs Fischer. The teddy's head sits inside a lamp, and the piece is known as… Lamp Bear

- Small Lie, a massive wooden sculpture by American artist, KAWS, depicting a Pinocchio inspired, almost Micky Mouse looking character, whose shoulders are slumped like a child would stand after getting in trouble

- Another public artwork, that kids can play on, is a copper playground, which is also the name of the piece, created by another American sculptor, Tom Otterness

- And not to be outdone, nature gets a look in with a whole oasis of trees inside a building that resides in a desert outside a city of skyscrapers and football stadiums

After getting through transit security and finding out which gate the next leg of the journey was leaving from, I had a 3-hour 20-minute layover and then set off on another 6-hour 50-minute Qatar Airways QR39 flight into Charles De Gaulle Airport, Paris.

Arrived at 2:33pm local time and got through all the usual security arrival, customs and baggage reclaim by 3:46pm. And it turns out, I should have used my Aussie or UK passport, rather than my shiny new Irish one as the EU lines were quite long. Problem was that once I had joined a line, there was little scope of getting out and hopping over to another one that was empty.

Top tip - if you are UK, Australian, Canadian or Mexican, there is a dedicated lane just for you! It's been a while between that day and this but I still can't work out how those four nationalities go together. I mean, the AusCanUK I get, but AusCanUKMex seems a stretch.

Baggage reclaim took an age but eventually my Osprey transit covered backpack turned up. Oh, yes, I should mention that. A backpack has all sorts of straps and dangly bits that I was a bit concerned about being 'snagged' or ripped, and given the number of pockets etc, there is practically no way of securing the bag without having it wrapped. I considered the plastic-wrapping available at airports, but trying to get it off at the other end without a knife (which would have to be packed inside the bag) seemed to be a pain and certainly not the most sustainable option. I therefore decided to invest in what Osprey call the *Airporter*. Basically, it's a big bag that your backpack goes into which protects it in transit. It's also lockable and has a shoulder strap which makes carrying it easy.

Once it came off the carousel, a quick unlock of the combo padlock and the backpack was ready to wear. The Airporter itself folds into its own internal pocket so that it ends up slightly bigger than palm size. The weight is about 1kg, but again, I wasn't going to need it on the trek, so it was going to be shipped forward as well.

Once loaded up, I checked my surroundings, followed the signs and headed to the free shuttle train that would take me from Terminal 1 to Terminal 3. More signs led me to the ticket machines for the RER train to central Paris. A one-way ticket cost €11.80.

If you're worried about navigating it all, don't be. Signs were in English and French and each ticket machine had an attendant next to it who was very willing to do all of the 'button pushing'.

I did wonder about this as it wasn't my experience any other time I'd arrived into Paris. I assumed it was the Parisians getting prepared for the upcoming (now completed) Olympic Games due to be held in July 2024. It might have been. It may be that the attendants won't be there in the future, which is a shame as the time it took them to sort the ticket out was much faster than letting tourists struggle to find the 'English Button'. The guy at my ticket machine asked me, in English (after clocking the Aus flag on my shoulder) if I wanted a single or return and to what station.

"Single to Denfert Rochereau, merci."
Voila!

To be fair, he didn't say, Voila. He didn't say anything more. He looked bored, but he was very helpful. I paid and he handed me the ticket with a very French tilt of the head.

Let's take a minute to talk about paying… There are a wealth of top-up before you go cards and all manner of ways to pay for your trip abroad, the least frugal of which is to use a credit card and allow them to set the currency conversion rates for you on a daily basis. No doubt you can also extract large quantities of cash and carry it in a money belt, but really, would you?

My solution, (and remember, this is a do whatever you want, not a must do piece of advice) was to open a multi-currency account which comes with a multi-currency card. I use Wise, and found it really works for international travel.

And now, back to Paris...

Exiting the Denfert Rochereau Metro at 4:45pm, I stepped out onto a wide Parisian boulevard in a bright spring afternoon that was gently steaming. I thought it was from the earlier rain showers but within three steps I'd smelt the heady, sweet, revolting whiff of cigarette smoke. As I said, I'm a former smoker, but I now can't stand the smell of them. I'd forgotten how prevalent cigarette smoking still was in Paris. It took about five minutes to see more smokers here than I'd seen in Western Australia in a year. I decided, in an effort to get away from the grey clouds, that I would walk the last kilometre or so to the Citadines Hotel in Montparnasse, my first accommodation choice of the trip.

You already know the basic requirements: my own room, my own bathroom, but I was on a budget, so the criteria I used throughout (bar the rest days and the end in Santiago) were:

- Ensuite

- A rating on Booking.com (yes, there are other booking sites, but this was the one I lumped for) of at least 8 with regard to cleanliness. The whole bedbug thing had gotten to me...

- As close to and preferably under, €50 per night

That last point was going to be a problem in Paris, given that my main reason for being here was to get up early on the 4th of April and get to Montparnasse train station. To make that happen, I wanted a hotel within walking distance of the station and there were lots, but most of them were very (I mean VERY) expensive. I simply needed a bed for the night. I chose the Citadines. It is a good, 'nice', reasonable, adequate (chose your own adjective) hotel. It came in at three times the nightly 'budget'. C'est la vie, as they say in Paris.

After a quick shower and change of clothes, I headed back out and took a leisurely meander north to a place that I had a hankering to visit. *Le Select*, the legendary establishment made famous by Hemingway in *The Sun Also Rises*.

If you haven't read it, well, apparently it is a classic novel… Yeah, what can I tell you? My thoughts on the book are less complimentary, but of course that may well be down to me not being 'edumecated' enough to tell good from bad. After all, you are reading my writing and I (obviously) think it is well-written, in my own 'style' but I am sure classic scholars would disagree. My style, I hope, is more like a conversation between myself and you (to borrow from Bridgerton) Dear Reader… Hemingway's style is, well it is. I love his short stories, but man-dear his novels are hard work.

Anyway, I digress, which is also a style of mine in conversation and writing. As my wife says on so many occasions, mimicking a close friend who once advised me to, "Tell the short version, Hoops."

For now, all that matters about Hemingway and 'The Sun' is that the characters in the book head down to Spain, gravitating around Navarra / the Basque country, and of course Pamplona. They stay during the festival that includes the now infamous bull running. My journey was going to be well outside of that 'fiesta-time', but I would be passing through some of Ernest's haunts and thought that having a drink in the café-bar would be an appropriate starting point.

It also allowed me to catch up with an author friend of mine and her French husband. We'd only previously caught up online, so it was great to finally meet in person. Alas, Le Select no longer sells the Absinthe of the 1930's (probably just as well) so I had a beer instead.

Then it was off to the Metro and a quick jaunt to that most wonderful of Parisienne book shops, *Shakespeare and Company*.

They shut at 8pm so it was a rapid look around and a chat with one of their many Irish staff, before going across the road to the banks of the Seine for a look at the majesty of Our Lady of Paris, (usually just called Our Lady or Notre-Dame in French). She was still recovering from her disastrous fire but rising tall and strong once again, albeit shrouded in the modesty of scaffolding and screens to protect her scarred, and charred, dignity. There's little doubt a lot of work is being done, but if the ancient lady was in a race to be fit for the soon to be held Paris Olympics she wasn't going to make it. Large pieces were still missing from the silhouette once so familiar on the Parisienne skyline.

Turning away from the river I headed down the grand Boulevard St. Michel where Jake, Hemingway's protagonist from The Sun Also Rises had his flat. I continued to traipse through an evening whose sky drew darker while the lights of restaurants, creperies and bars grew brighter. It all looked so enticing that had I still smoked, I might have drawn up a chair and had a Galouises, coffee and crêpe. As it was, my lungs thanked me for not doing that, and my jet lag told me I needed sleep.

It was now 22:22, and I had made it through days 1 and 2. I sank into a very comfortable bed and remained awake for about an hour or so. Finally, I slept, only to waken again at 3.33. Seemed whilst all the numbers were aligning, my jetlag was not going to encourage me to rest. I got up and looked out on a rainy morning in Paris, watching and waiting for the clock to tick around and for the *sun to rise*.

Steps walked:
Day 1: 13,976 and
Day 2: 16,392

Day Minus-2

April 4th 2024
Montparnasse, Paris - Saint-Jean-Pied-de-Port
Planned distance: 823km
Steps planned to be walked: Again, not that many

The sun hadn't managed to muster much in the way of a rise and the rain was still falling, when I exited the Citadines Hotel and walked 200 metres to Gare Montparnasse. It meant that I got to test the built-in rain cover for my backpack, as I still hadn't caught up with the poncho I hoped to buy.

The big Paris railway stations are just that: Big. Montparnasse has three, maybe four levels and 28 platforms, 24 of which are accessed through the main Halls 1 and 2 which was where I found myself. The halls had three main screens within sight of where I stood, all of which showed dissimilar information. Turns out there are local trains and express trains and some run by one company and some run by another. After a few minutes I managed to find the one I was looking for. The TGV train to Bayonne at 7:04am. By the by, what is it with French timetables? It's always 03 or 07 or 24 minutes past or to the hour. Never on the hour or in multiples of 5 minutes? I don't know why that is and it slightly bugs me.

Having completed my walk to the station, orientated myself and sorted out that I now had a half hour to kill, I got a croissant and coffee in my best French, to which the young lady behind the counter replied in perfect English.

At 6:55am I was starting to get a little concerned that the train's platform still hadn't been displayed on screen. The concourse was thronged now and a lot of the throngees (if that isn't a word, it should be) were milling about with backpacks, hiking boots and a general air of potential pilgrims. There seemed to be a couple of larger groups and their backpacks were already adorned with quite a lot of religious motifs and 'patches'. They looked like they knew exactly where they were going and I figured I might do worse than follow along with them, but they weren't heading anywhere either.

There was a definite air of discomfort from the knowledge of only having a few minutes to get on the train, and not knowing where the train was. Whispers started on the concourse. Pilgrims were getting restless… I decided to sit to one side and observe, drinking my coffee and figuring, well, it has to turn up at some point.

It did. At 06:57 the platform was displayed and we were informed that the train would be leaving at precisely 07:04 (if I caught the Montparnasse Station announcer correctly).

Way to go… Coffee and croissant wrapper in the nearest bin, backpack heaved on and a forced march to the gate, where a hundred people squeezed down into two by twos, ark-like. Show the e-ticket get on down the platform, find coach 12, board, go up a flight of stairs, find seat 71. Hoik backpack into luggage compartment right next to the seat I had specifically booked online yonks before through the SNCF Connect website. Relax. Look at watch. 07:01, heaps of time.

"Bonjour?"

I looked up to a well-dressed guy a bit younger than me.

"Bonjour," I said, a bit confused as there was no seat next to me. Seat 71 was a single at the end of the carriage, so it wasn't like he was asking me to shift so he could sit next to me.

"Something in French that I didn't catch… dans ma place!" he said, accompanied by a pointing finger at the seat.

"Non," I said, with my accompanying finger pointing at the phone I still held with my e-ticket displayed on it.

He peered. A light of realisation came on. I relaxed.

He said, "Something in French."

I shrugged, in French. My idea of tourists speaking the language of the country they are in, disappeared rapidly. "You speak English? I do not understand."

"You are on ze wrong train. Zis is coach douze, back train. You are going to Bayonne. Coach douze front train. Aller, aller!"

Lots of words came to mind, most I am sure would not have required much in the way of translation.

I got up and leapt off the train. On the platform at irregular distances were uniformed TGV people. Each one I neared took that moment to turn and get on the train. There was no talking to their backs. Instead, I counted off the coach numbers on each door. As I rounded the 'bend' of the platform, I realised just how long this train was. Eventually, with quite a lot of adrenaline 'sweating' through me on this humid, sodden, Parisienne morning, I got to where the numbers stopped going up and reset themselves to 11. Another carriage to 12, in and up a flight of stairs to seat 71. Backpack in the luggage compartment, seat taken. Check watch. As I looked at my wrist, the display clicked over from 7:03 to 7:04 and the train moved.

Turns out that a strange time of 7:04 does not mean an 'about that' time, it means precisely at 7:04. Like some Sci-fi train driving automaton pressed go as the seconds clicked to 07:04:00.

I took a minute or three, or ten, to calm myself.

Once my heart rate was back to a semblance of normality, the rest of the journey was quite superb. The onboard wifi and accompanying webpage (link given on the overhead information display) were excellent. Seriously, the webpage showed every detail of the journey and had a pre-order method for food and drinks from the restaurant car which meant you ordered and paid then sauntered up after five minutes or so and they handed it to you.

The wifi was handy as about an hour into the journey the SNCF App informed me that the train I was due to take from Bayonne to Saint-Jean-Pied-de-Port (StJPdP) was not running. I could get my money back by clicking, then I could re-book, but the next train was going to be that night, maybe.

Travelling at 317 Kph down through France was not the best place to consider options. Rather sit back, enjoy the ride and the view, and work it out when I got there. At 11:03 (precisely) we pulled into Bayonne. Within a few minutes of milling about the concourse of a wide open and sunny station area, it became clear that no trains would be running and that instead, a rail replacement bus service was going to be laid on. Tickets would still be valid.

I had an hour to wait, so wandered out of the station and into the most glorious spring day. Sunshine, blues skies, a few fluffy white clouds meandering across the azure and about forty other backpackers meandering across the town square. I opted to go for a short dander about the town, circled back at the river and found a café that served alcohol. Taking a seat outside in the balmy 20c midday sun I enjoyed the quiet of the world as it passed by whilst I sipped on a gorgeous white wine, whose name and grape variety were my standard order when in Europe, 'blanc de maison'. Can't go far wrong with a house white on the continent! I assessed that, so far, the Camino was going quite well.

Eventually the hour neared and I ventured back to the carpark in front of the train station, to find a large coach waiting. Two drivers conversed in French outside it and as I approached one asked, "Saint Jean?" (But he pronounced it more like, San Shon).

I replied, "Oui." Yeah, I know… I'm practically fluent!

Backpack in the luggage compartment, me on board an already half-full coach. I was overcome with a memory of being on a bus destined for high school, albeit this one was a lot nicer than the old 'Ulsterbusses' I had used back then. Obviously, with that in mind, I went all the way to the back seats, just like I used to on those high school trips.

Happily ensconced, I decided to check in on comms with my two Camino companions. How did I do that you ask? Well, you didn't but

I'll tell you anyway. I had an e-sim downloaded before I left Australia. I used Airalo. It cost me $100 Aud for 50gb valid for 90 days (which was more than I needed but the other option was 30 days which was less than I needed). All in all, it worked flawlessly. It was only for data, but with WhatsApp for calls I didn't need actual SMS or call time.

I knew Popper was already in StJPdP along with his wife, Michelle. Paddy was en route from the USA.

I checked Facebook.

Paddy had posted only five minutes earlier that he was in Bayonne and about to get on a bus!

I looked back up the rows of seats but couldn't see him, so I rang his number. A phone began to chirp twenty seats away. A head rose up from where it had previously been reading a book.

"Ian! How are you?"

"Turn around and I'll tell ya!"

And that was how two boys who last saw each other on that afore-mentioned high school bus, met again!

Paddy's now a tall fella, around six-foot, (he obviously continued growing quite a bit since school – unlike me). He's also tanned in a way that did not come from Northern Ireland, but was acquired over four decades of travelling, first in bar work and hospitality, then in real estate. He's lived in various places, including London and now resides just outside Boston, Massachusetts. He left our hometown of Larne in 1987, but I hadn't seen or talked to him in person since 1982. Forty-two years and yet, as he dropped his sturdy frame down beside me on the bus, it was like we'd spoken yesterday.

I don't think my accent has changed much from my NI days, but I did once work with the USAF for almost a year and I found a US twang began to assert itself on certain words. I think the Irish and US accents share a kinship borne of long lines of migration stretching back over centuries. My accent reverted quickly once I had stopped the close working contact, but Paddy, who has lived there for longer than he lived at home, now has the distinct cadence and burr of Bostonian in his vowels. He used to have a nickname in school, but when not called by it, he was always known as Paddy. Nowadays, in his working life in the US he goes by Patrick, yet he fell straight back into Paddy as soon as we started talking.

He and his wife had been thinking about the Camino a few weeks before Popper reached out. He took it as an uncanny, 'sign' that it was time to do the walk. Definitely more religious in his outlook than 'heathen-me', he was looking forward to the solace, the opportunity for reflection and the potential of visiting some beautiful churches and cathedrals along the way.

As we chatted, the bus started off on an hour's journey through idyllic scenery that showcased the majesty of the Pyrenees' foothills and the beauty of nature's design. A fast-flowing river with white crested rapids ran down alongside the road which twisted and turned ever upwards, surrounded by towering, lusciously green hills and Swiss-chocolate-box villages. The rail line that we should have been travelling on, ran parallel in places, like a giant's toy with exquisitely painted and perfectly modelled station houses and signal boxes. It needed a steam locomotive chuffing its way along the tracks and a background score of uplifting classical music to complete the scene. My imagination added them for effect.

After a few final turns and a short transit through a town, which I recognised from long pondering of YouTube videos, the bus stopped at StJPdP's railway station. Grabbing our gear, we walked up a small hill, messaged Popper who was in the town already and within ten minutes we had met in the lobby of the Hotel Itzalpea.

This is Basque country and on the border of France and Spain, so you have a choice of potential languages to use. Needless to say, the staff in the hotel spoke perfectly fluent English. (Yeah, I had learnt a few phrases in Basque too. Seemed a good thing to do… My oh my it's a different language, but so intriguing).

Like me, Popper hadn't seen Paddy since leaving school. Popper and I had only met once in the intervening four decades. Yet again, it felt seamless. The idea of sitting in the sun and catching up over a beer, or five was appealing, but we had things to do first.

Popper had been in town for a few days. His wife, Michelle, also wanted to do the Camino but she had determined to walk it solo, as a personal challenge. They'd arrived in France from their home in Queensland and having acclimatised a little, Michelle had set off up into the mountains yesterday. Popper walked with her to the Refuge Orisson, where she went on and he came back down to StJPdP. I say back down as it is, most definitely, down. Quite a lot down.

Orisson is about 8km from StJPdP, which sounds like a walk in the park, but it is an 800m elevation change. Now, the problem is, if you have no experience of walking up the Pyrenees, (and we didn't) that doesn't sound too bad. Popper begged (and I mean, stressed a lot with quite forceful language) to tell us that in fact, 800m up in just under 8km distance was ROUGH!

"It's brutal in places, boys. Seriously. I don't think you know what you have in store."

With the warning tucked away, he escorted us up to the Camino office. We timed it fortuitously, as when we got to the door there were only three peregrinos in the queue. Paddy and I were quickly seen by one of the four volunteers who explained what the Pilgrim Credential or Pilgrim Passport was.

In the Middle Ages, the faithful would carry a scalloped shell as proof of their journey and, arriving at Santiago, they'd receive blessings for having completed their pilgrimage. However, human-nature being what it ever was, unscrupulous types started selling shells to those who hadn't actually completed the walk. Tisk Tisk! Another way had to be found.

Well, that's one story that surrounds the certification. Suffice to say that the passport issued free in Saint Jean, and also available to buy online from anywhere in the world, has a simplified map of the route, a few explanatory paragraphs about the Way and a concertina of four, double-sided pages, each with eight blank squares. That's a total of sixty-four places that you can have stamps (and the date) applied from each town you stay in, and other intervening places if you want to. You **have** to get it stamped at each overnight stop, and from Sarria onwards into Santiago (the last 115 kms), you **have** to get it stamped at least twice a day.

Once in Santiago, the passport is presented to the Pilgrim's Office and in return you are granted the Compostela Certificate, written in Latin and issued by the Church to all pilgrims. The minimum requirement to get one is to walk 100km (or cycle, or ride a horse for 200km), to Santiago.

There are some changes to this requirement being introduced in 2025, so make sure to check it out before you go.

The Compostela is issued free to all pilgrims. You can also pay €3 (three euros) for the Certificate of Distance, a document issued by the Chapter of the Cathedral of Santiago that certifies the number of kilometres you have travelled, whatever your starting point might be. Traditionally, pilgrimage was calculated from leaving your own home, but I figured 'Australia' might be a stretch, so mine would be StJPdP.

Lastly, for anyone fretting about how you get these certificates back home without being crushed in your backpack, (like I did for unfeasibly stupid amounts of time) well fear not, a couple of euros more also buys you a neat little cardboard document tube. But that was all in the future. We were still a long way from finishing.

Back in the office in Saint Jean were versions of the passport in every language imaginable, but they'd run out of English ones when I got there, so I opted for the French version. Like most 'proper' pilgrimage 'things', these were given freely, and you could also take a traditional scalloped shell to carry on your journey, but donations were kindly accepted.

Paddy and I collected our credentials, (Popper had gotten his when Michelle and he had first arrived). We made a donation, picked a shell each and left the office to find a queue of about fifty pilgrims stretching down the hill and waiting patiently to get in. Lucky us.

Across the street was the *Boutique du Pelerin*, a place I needed to go to and one that is run by the affable, enthusiastic, and extremely efficient owner, Pierre.

You'll recall that I wanted to buy an Altus Poncho but had no chance of getting one in Australia. After a few web searches, I found that they were sold in the Boutique du Pèlerin in StJPdP. Great, I thought, saves me carrying it all the way there, but what happens if they don't have any? I decided to email them. I put my request through Google translate and included the French version as well. I got this reply later the same day:

"Bonjour Ian, thank you for trust and order with us.

I put immediately aside for you a Medium/Large blue ALTUS poncho until your arrival in Saint Jean Pied de Port April 4th. You will pay only arriving here. If you have any other question about hiking equipment, don't hesitate to ask us.

Good preparation for your pilgrimage and see you in few weeks....

Best regards. Cordiales salutations.

Pierre"

It was now the 4th of April. I'd emailed them on the 1st of March with no communication in the intervening weeks. I walked into an extremely busy shop. Imagine pilgrims everywhere! Paddy was visible only by his height as he perused sturdy walking sticks. Others milled around inside and out, surveying the full-to-the-brim-with-stock store. I approached a man standing in the middle of the swirl (he had a name tag of Pierre, so I guessed he worked there) and said, in my best French, that I had reserved a poncho.

"Ian?"

A little surprised I said, "Eh, yes."

To be completely honest, I looked down at my own chest to see if I had somehow put a name tag on without remembering. I hadn't.

"Good, good. A medium-large blue Altus Poncho. I have it here."

I don't know what systems Pierre has in place to recall my name and my order a month after I emailed him, whilst running a store that is 'bunged' full of customers on a daily basis, and summoning that information in an instant, but whatever his magic is, it works.

He even showed me how best to get the Altus on and off whilst wearing a full pack. Bravo Pierre!! In thanks, I paid an extra €3 and got one of their more appealing, and slightly smaller shells which bore a red symbol on its surface.

On first glance it was simply a cross, but on closer examination, it looked more like a sword. I discovered it was the 'Cross of St James' and is represented as a red cross *flory* or flowered cross over a white field, and the shape is actually the blade of a sword. The military, red sword-cross of St James of Compostela is one of Galicia's oldest national symbols and was adopted as the symbol of the Military Order of Santiago, a Christian knighthood founded in the 12th century in the kingdoms of Castile and Portugal for patrolling their borders with Muslim Spain.

I, like I imagine most folk do, carried it because it looked 'pretty'. I tucked the bigger, plainer shell inside a pocket and clipped this one onto my pack. It would go with me, as well as three small clipped-on flags. The Province of Ulster flag, the RAF ensign and the Australian flag. Between them they summed up my journey so far and the shell would represent the journey I was starting out on. Yeah, well, it was all symbolic, no one other than me would get the meaning of it and if it seemed a bit of overkill, I blame the jetlag.

The rest of the day was spent with a small wander around the picture-book village whose red-tiled roofs, cobbled streets and mountainous backdrops made the heart and soul feel good.

Eventually, we took a table in the small alfresco seating area out front of the Hotel Itzalpea. It was mid-afternoon. The sun was shining, the temperature in the mid-20s, and the beers kept arriving. Bearing in mind all three of us had been on different continents a few days before, and we were all 'allegedly' in some form of training for the Camino, our ability and enthusiasm to order another round was undiminished.

By late evening we had reminisced and played catch-up in the way one does with old school friends who haven't seen each other for forty years. We had filled in a few more blanks about what we'd been up to since 1982, when we'd left high school.

Popper's plans to train as a marine engineer, scuppered by the downturn in the British Merchant Fleet. Subsequently becoming a welder and going to New Zealand with $200 in his pocket. Later moving to Australia, and now, after many qualifications and a vast array of experience in some of the biggest engineering projects on the planet, he runs his own international Project Services company.

Paddy moved to London and worked in hospitality, then onto America doing the same, before getting into the building game. A while later he combined his customer relations skills and his building knowledge to become a realtor in the Greater Boston area. Now he is one of the most experienced, knowledgeable and successful real estate agents in New England.

And me. Joined up at eighteen, served as an air communications technician, then commissioned as an Intelligence Officer. After my 'retirement' from the Service I moved to Australia, started a training consultancy, then wrote some novels and now I run a publishing company whilst also being an editor, ghost writer and book festival organiser.

We toasted the teachers who had told all three of us we would amount to nothing. We also toasted the ones who had been a little more positive in their outlook.

More beers were consumed.

Eventually, in the calm dark of a French-Basque spring night that despite being cloudless, was still comfortably warm, we wrapped it up.

Tomorrow was a planned rest day to allow a little more time for acclimatisation and jet lag recovery. I figured I could add hangover recovery to that too.

That said, my room was on the first floor up a flight of relatively steep steps that I managed to conquer with no ill effect. I also had enough wherewithal to record the steps I'd managed and to properly appreciate a double bed and a decent shower. I fell asleep at 11pm.

Steps walked: 9,825

Day Minus-1

April 5th 2024
Rest Day: Saint-Jean-Pied-de-Port
Planned distance: 0km
Steps planned to be walked: As few as possible
Planned alcohol consumption: As little as possible

Surprisingly, I woke up without any trace of a hangover. Unsurprisingly, I woke up at 04:12 thanks to time zone befuddlement. I was reminded of the line from *Good Morning, Vietnam*, "What's the 'oh' stand for? Oh my God that's early!" I eventually gave up trying to get back to sleep, got up, had a shower, and by 06:00 was out for a walk around Saint-Jean. Turns out quite a lot of places are open in the town at that hour, including a coffee shop!

Climbing up the steps of the old town's battlements I watched the sun's gentle rise into a clear sky. As the eastern horizon brightened, I looked south-southwest, to where our path tomorrow would take us. Somehow, being up on the town's battlements, higher than ground-level, made the mountains loom larger still. The Pyrenees, initially a darker black than the lightening sky, began to take form and substance, revealing the greens and browns of fields and copses, and quite a few residences that prompted the thought, "How do you build a house up there?" Each one of the houses, tiny clones of one another, with white walls and red roofs, looked false, like the giant's toy train set from yesterday. Too perfect to be real. Perhaps it was all an elaborate film set with pristine houses on pristine mountain slopes. If it was a film set, my only wish was that the set-designer had made those mountains a bit smaller. Ah well, their true nature would be revealed in less than twenty-four hours.

I headed back to the hotel to partake in a continental breakfast consisting of bread, jam, coffee, and a few slices of cheese. Joined by Paddy, we spent a half hour chatting to Alex, a German guy who had been a soldier in Afghanistan. He said he was doing the Camino for himself, and for some friends who hadn't made it home.

The day was spent pottering. It included a trip to the local Carrefour supermarket to stock up on whatever we needed. Turned out, not a lot, although I do like a stroll around a 'foreign' supermarket. So much to see and go, "Ohh, that's clever," or "Oh, they look nice," and so little time to buy it all and eat it! I ended up getting, just so we didn't look out of place, some boiled sweets, a few protein bars and an apple that looked as red and rosy as the one the witch gave Snow White. Honestly, I've never seen such an 'Appley' looking apple.

Deciding we couldn't seize up completely, we went for a lazy walk along the River Nive (more correctly The *Nive de Béhérobie*, or main stream) heading southeast out of the town until we got dead-ended and had to turn back. It was on this walk that for the first, but not last time, Popper displayed an amazing talent at spotting fish in a river. He's a keen fisherman and travels internationally for his hobby, but his ability to spot a catch was astounding.

Between the walk, lunch in one of the myriad of eateries and generally chilling out, I dropped a bag off to the Express Bourricot service. This was the bag of kit I needed in the UK after the Camino as well as the Airporter bag. For €70 the next time I would see it and the 4kg it weighed, would be in Santiago. Yes, there are cheaper courier methods once you get into Spain, but that would have meant lugging the extra weight over the mountains.

Now… let's take a moment to talk about carrying backpacks and how much they weigh. If you are thinking of doing the Camino, as I have mentioned before, be cautious about the forums and advice pages, for as well as some nasty comments, a lot of people on the sites seem to be terribly focused on the weight of their kit. Yes, light is better than heavy but try not to become obsessed about it. That said, carrying an extra 4kg of stuff I didn't need for the next month seemed a bit ridiculous, so I decided to send it on its merry way.

The staff in the office spoke perfect English and switched to it effortlessly, so another opportunity to practice my French slipped by. Perhaps they wanted to practice their English. Perhaps they heard my atrocious accent and dived in to save the soul of their mother tongue. I suspect the latter.

After a peaceful, relaxed and chatty day, we went for dinner at a restaurant called *Cidrerie Hurrup Eta Klik,* which specialises in Basque cuisine. A wonderful, almost cosy, ambience led to another evening of stories and reminiscing between the three of us, but less booze. The food was superb. I ordered one of the specialities, Basque Chicken, a hotpot of chicken and rice, olives and peppers, soaking in a stunning sauce and given a hint of spice with chorizo sausage and paprika. It was good, although at one point I distinctly remember thinking that the sauce made the chicken look a little pink. It was a bit off-putting, but never mind, it tasted great and the house white was a refreshing accompaniment.

We steered clear of talking about the Pyrenees and the challenges of tomorrow. Personally, my lack of training on appropriate terrain was niggling at the back of my mind, but there hadn't been a lot I could do about it. The highest peak in Western Australia was lower than what we'd climb on our first day and it was, 'the wrong type of hill'; being much shorter and steeper (with high steps) rather than the rolling ranges of the Pyrenees. Our plan was distilled down to, keep putting one foot in front of the other, it's not a race and weeping pitifully will be permitted. We wrapped things up and had an early night. Tomorrow would be a big day for sure. What we didn't know then was just how much it would test us.

Steps walked: 15,077

THE WAY

Day 1

April 6th 2024
Saint-Jean-Pied-de-Port - Roncesvalles
Planned distance travelled: 24.7km
Steps planned to be walked: 30,000 (guesstimate)

I woke early and was down for breakfast at 06:00, except there was no hotel breakfast to be had at that hour. The only other person up was a Canadian lady from Quebec.

Now, for the first few days of the Camino I didn't know that my notes, and ultimately this book, would focus on the people I met, so starting out, I didn't ask permission to use their names. Where I did, great. Where I didn't I'll either leave them nameless, or like here, make one up... We shall call this lady, Anna.

As she was sorting out her pack, she told me that she was newly retired, loved hiking but wanted to save doing the Canadian trails until the day when no one would provide her international travel insurance. Until then she would do as many walks overseas as she could. Today was also her start day on the Camino and she was looking forward to it after a long build-up of planning and preparation.

I agreed and told her of Paddy, Popper and myself. A year and a few days since the first message and now, here we were, on the threshold of the first proper step. We both took in the World Map mounted in the hotel's small dining area. It had pins marking the homes of pilgrims who'd set out on what we were about to do. I reflected that most of the pins came from what would once have been called, 'First World Nations'. The more acceptable definition nowadays, states:

the 'First World' is generally thought of as the capitalist, industrial, wealthy, and developed countries. This includes the countries of North America and Western Europe, Japan, South Korea, Australia, and New Zealand.

It fitted the map well. There were a few, no more than five, outlying pins in some South American countries, some in Mexico, a scattering in South Africa and one or two in Southeast Asian nations such as Singapore and Vietnam, but the rest were clustered in those capitalist, industrial, wealthy, and developed countries. I know it was only one hotel of many and not necessarily reflective of the people who would be staying in hostels and other types of accommodation. I also knew that scientifically it wouldn't merit a decent or unbiased sample size, but it nonetheless made me reflect on the nature of this new type of 'Pilgrimage'.

I added my own pin to Western Australia and a collective one for the three wanderers to mark Larne, Northern Ireland. Anna added hers to Quebec. She finished her coffee, slung her backpack over her shoulders, picked up her trekking poles and bade me farewell.

Paddy and Popper joined me soon after, adding their own pins to their adopted homes and then we started our Camino Francés at 07:00 in the pre-dawn darkness. We got as far as the other side of the road before we found a café that was open, where we stopped to get take-away coffees. No point in being martyrs for the fun of it.

Then we set off again, turned left through the Porte de France onto the Rue de France, south on the main Rue de la Citadelle and exited St Jean through the historic Porte Notre-Dame.

We were in good spirits. Popper had a walking staff made of the finest, honey-blonde chestnut wood. Paddy's, that he'd bought two days earlier, was darker, almost Gandalf-like, and I had my trekking poles. As instructed by quite a few sources, we didn't use the sticks whilst in the confines of the urban area, as it drives the locals nuts with the tip tapping of passing souls. Almost silently, we walked out of St Jean and headed for the Spanish settlement of Roncesvalles, with some 20+kms (and the western Pyrenees) between us and it.

There are two routes to get from StJPdP to Roncesvalles. A lot of sources can provide the finer detail of both, but basically it comes down to a high road and a low road. I had desperately wanted to do the high road. I sought the test of the mountains and I hoped it would be clear so I could appreciate the vistas I had seen on so many videos. It is called Route Napoleon, named as it was used to transport artillery for Napoleon's armies (he never set foot on it) and it is closed over the winter and in periods of bad weather. It had been opened for the first time in 2024 on the 1st of April and then closed again for a couple of days after a heavy snowfall. Reopening again on the 5th (just in time for Michelle to use it) meant that we could also go that way. As could the scattered bunch of others who had set out in the early morning. Within 500 metres we had received our first few greetings of, "Buen Camino", a phrase that would become so much a part of our lives for the next month.

The rise in the road started almost immediately and became a slog up a steep incline that kept going for a kilometre or two. Within that first half an hour we had figured out that Paddy was tall with a long stride, I was not but walked quickly and Popper walked slightly slower. We decided that we'd walk at our own pace, keep an eye out for each other, stop and bunch up every so often and keep WhatsApp open just in case.

Two kilometres in and the most spectacular dark orange sunrise with flashes of yellow and crimson lit up the sky behind us. Another pilgrim ahead had stopped to take in the view and offered to take the first photo of the three of us on the Camino. He got carried away and took a dozen. I'm glad he did as the sunrise was worth it. My torchlight, fixed to my shoulder straps, was still on and the resultant photos look like I have a glowing apparition affixed to me.

By the time we had passed 3k, my legs and back were getting used to it and I was thinking, it wasn't too bad as long as we kept our pace and rhythm. We got to Orisson (**7.7**k and 800 m elevation) at 10am and although definitely a reflection of Popper's words, "Brutal in places," we had achieved it and felt good. We took a break, had a drink and something to eat, checked our feet for blisters, of which there were none and started off again. I did think, after eating a croissant, my stomach felt a bit queasy. Never mind, press on.

Ultimately, it would be a total of 18.7kms of steep and some very steep inclines before we reached the highest elevation and yet, until the 10km mark, (at 900m elevation) we were making great progress. The day had settled into a perfect combination of not too hot, not too cold, a clear sky that had revealed itself after the breath-taking sunrise, amazing views of rolling peaks and deep valleys, all topped off with friendly banter in good company.

The only real issue was when we stopped for a break, and I ate my 'Snow White' apple. No sooner had it gone down, than it came back up. I drank some water. It did the same. I felt ill and my stomach was doing somersaults. Paddy looked at me and said, in a caring, nursing manner, "Hell, Ian, you're as white as a ghost."

I recalled the chicken from the night before. Perhaps it hadn't been the sauce making it look pink after all. Ah f… for goodness' sake, I thought to myself. Halfway up the Pyrenees is not the place to discover you have a touch of food poisoning. I fished in my pack and found some Imodium. Being sick was one thing, but being *otherwise inconvenienced* on a mountain was quite another. I took a few more sips of water and advised that we should keep going. As if there was much alternative.

When my phone beeped at me to mark 10km we were, despite my upset stomach, in great spirits and felt fine. That beep was heard as the first gust of wind was felt. By 11km the 'breeze' had picked up considerably. By 13km it was gusting to about 50 kph. By 15km it was a sustained 80 kph.

Now… walking up hill from the 900m elevation that we had reached relatively easily, to the approximate 1400m elevation which marked the top of the ascent became increasingly torturous. The headwind was unceasing (I can only explain it as walking forward with a determined person pushing against your shoulders) and the particular horror of 'death by a hundred false peaks' came into play. You know the type of thing, topping a peak, and in the last few steps uttering the phrase, "Oh we made it," only to then find another one rising up in the distance. We had that, on repeat. A lot of times…

The worst instance of this false finish was at 15kms next to the Croix de Thibault, when the road seems to flatten but the Camino pathway goes to the right and straight up another rise. A big one. The break we took at that point coincided with me trying to digest a protein bar. After a few minutes I figured I was over the worst. I was wrong and proceeded to throw up, narrowly missing a passing elderly Korean lady. She jumped niftily out of the way. I was impressed at her nimbleness. She was not impressed by me at all. To be fair, she also looked a bit shocked as when she jumped sideways, the wind almost carried her off the hill. Eventually, we slogged on and made the top. About 8km to go.

Paddy and Popper suggested I took half an hour to see if the nausea (and perhaps the wind) would subside. Seemed like a good idea, after all, the rest of the journey was downhill. Except, it wasn't.

It turns out that as Spain pushed into France 150 million years ago, some of the downward slopes went too far down and so, to get back up to where we needed to be, we had to climb again. And then go down again and then up again. The wind got stronger. By which stage the banter had reduced and my bright idea (for sadly it was all my idea) to start in StJPdP for the 'challenge' could have become an acceptable case for the defence if Popper and Paddy had been so inclined. Thankfully they weren't.

At 20km, as we got to the last of the ridges and passed banks of iced snow left over from a few days beforehand, our phones sounded an emergency alert warning of the onset of an even worse storm and advising all people to get off the mountains.

By now I was feeling a bit better, as in I hadn't thrown up for a couple of hours, but the conditions were getting tougher. We took it a hundred metres at a time. One foot after the other, breaks when we needed them. After a total distance of 26.17km, more than half of it against storm force winds, we arrived into Roncesvalles at 18:23. It had taken us 11 hrs and 23 minutes.

The stats from my Garmin confirmed that in fact we had made good progress… when we'd been moving. Almost half the elapsed time, 5 hours 45 minutes, had been recorded as us 'moving' with the remainder being spent in enforced breaks. The wind literally forced us at times to take one pace forward, two back and rest. As for that wind, the highest recorded gust against us was 89.3km/h. I'd later discover it had ripped off the Aussie and RAF flags from my back-pack. The Camino shell and the flag of the Province of Ulster had hung on in there. I figured there was something symbolic in that, but I was too knackered to contemplate it.

Was it the hardest physical thing I have ever done? No. That still goes to carrying a very heavy 'dummy-dead-mannequin' on a 12-mile route march through mud in Rutland, but this came close and 30+ years later and with a touch of food poisoning. It was certainly not a dander in the hills. But at least it hadn't rained and we achieved our destination. Roncesvalles, home to one of the biggest albergues on the Camino and one that, regardless of your arrival time, you have to wait in a queue to get into, be assigned a bed and grab a hot shower, if there is enough hot water left. This early in the season it would probably have been fine, but when we arrived at almost half past six, there were still pilgrims waiting to get in.

Thankfully, in a moment of foresight, we three had decided that after what might be 'a relatively hard day' (oh we had been naïve when we'd had that conversation months before), we should have an easy night and so had booked the neighbouring, Hotel Roncesvalles.

I took a magnificent, wonderous, soul-restoring shower that lasted about 30 minutes and was equally happy when I remembered we had also decided that tomorrow and the next day should be 'light' days. Keep the legs moving, but not far. Only 11kms each. A couple of recovery days of sorts.

Popper and Paddy went for dinner. I drank tea in my room and stayed close to the 'facilities'. On reflection, Basque Chicken the night before starting one's Camino might have been a mistake, but it made for a better story, so every cloud… Before turning in, I checked the stats:

Steps walked: 35,039 steps (total steps for the day)
Camino distance travelled: 26.17kms (point to point on the Camino)
Starting Elevation: 161m
Highest Elevation: 1,425m
Total elevation ascents: 1,564m
Total descents: 772m
Pitifully weeping: 0.

Day 2

April 7th 2024
Roncesvalles - Viscarret-Guerendiáin
Planned distance: 11km
Planned steps: Less than yesterday

I woke refreshed and happy. Legs were in good nick, feet were fine. Aches and pains, none. Tummy still a bit up and down. Literally. But it was a relaxed start which saw us taking buffet breakfast at the Hotel Roncesvalles (sumptuous in the Spanish cheese, meat, bread style) and an actual use of my language skills as we tried to get some *mantequilla* (butter). Turns out the Navarra / Basque region of Spain (and to a lesser extent elsewhere) was not that keen on butter. Olive oil they could do, strawberry jam they could do, but butter was obviously an odd request. The young waitress gave us a look like we'd asked for, "Caviar and be quick about it." I double checked I had actually asked for butter. I had. It was not forthcoming.

We checked-out at 11, walked a few metres to get the obligatory photo at the road sign which says, Santiago de Compostela 790, and then we took a slow walk for 11.66km 'down' towards Viscarret-Guerendiáin. Down being a relative term as nothing is truly down in this part of Navarra. This is still the foothills of a mountain range and there were a couple of steep hills, but mere pimples compared to yesterday. Also, in an attempt to counter erosion, some of the steeper parts are paved on this stretch. Crucially though, there was no wind. At all. It was the serenest of days.

About 3k from our start point we arrived in Burguete (Auritz) made famous by Hemingway staying there many times and featuring it in The Sun Also Rises. The village greets the traveller with brightly painted murals announcing itself and celebrating the nature, wildlife and heritage of the place. As we walked up the main street it was, like one of those old westerns, quiet. Too quiet. Then I remembered it was Sunday.

As I was musing that a coffee was unlikely to be on the cards we saw a lady crossing the road and opening the door to a restaurant. A quick test of my Spanish later and we were in being served. I ordered the stereotypical, *Café con Leche* (coffee with milk, think of it as a short latte) so synonymous with Camino walkers. Got to admit, I drink a lot of coffee normally, but whether it was the aftermath of the 'Basque Chicken' or just the thought of wanting something lighter, that solitary café con leche was one of my last coffees on the Camino.

Post break and sauntering through the quiet streets, we got about thirty metres before Paddy realised he'd forgotten his stick. Back we went, which was fortuitous because it was only then I realised I had walked past the *Hostal* that apparently Hemmingway used to stay in. He shared a passion with Popper, being a mad-keen trout fisherman and used to come here regularly. In *The Sun*, he has Jake Barnes, stay in it with a friend, Bill Gorton, before they continue on to see the bullfights in Pamplona.

Stick retrieved, we three friends set off to follow in their fictional footsteps. A few minutes later our phones pinged with a WhatsApp message. It may seem like there were only three of us (at this point) on the Way, but that's not true. Since the earliest stages of preparation, through to yesterday, today, and for the rest of our Camino, WhatsApp would ping at regular intervals, with either Paddy, Popper or me sharing things, or (and vitally) messages from Mark, Michael and Gerry back 'home' in Northern Ireland. On occasions, their messages were more important than they could know. The occasional, "Looking good, lads" when we posted a photo, or more usually, acerbic banter and awful jokes that kept us buoyed up when the going was tough, boring, bland or all three.

I shan't be able to recreate them all, but here's a small flavour.

If you are into church, then you know lighting candles is a 'thing'. We got this a few days before starting out:

Mark: Just back from Mass. I got a few candles for the mountain climbers.

Me: Unless Candles is the name of a donkey you have hired, I think you need to try harder.

A few days in:

Mark: How's the legs today?

Michael: (from his couch at home): Mine are fine.

Gerry: (From his vaulted position of being by far the tallest amongst us): Ian's are still short.

And, always at the right time, Gerry would pop up with a joke or a funny meme. Mostly they were rubbish (only kidding Gerry) but they did make us laugh. It was probably the fatigue. As an example:

Gerry: How do you know what the weather is like on top of a mountain?

Us:...?

Gerry: Climate!

Our basecamp supporters were, and still are, appreciated more than they probably realise. Cheers lads.

Passing through Espinal at 6.6km we pressed on for Viscarret and for the rest of the day were surrounded by green pastures, bright carpets of wildflowers, dandelions and daisies, accompanied by a background score of tweeting songbirds and trickling brooks. The narrow pathways and general landscapes reminded us of locations near Larne. Our conversations played over the walks and cycle rides we had taken as kids, back in the days when we were let out in the early morning and expected back when it got dark. I once heard an expression that our generation (Gen x) had been raised by parents whose parenting skills were akin to compassionate abandon, or perhaps, loving neglect. Without rehashing the whole gen debate, personally I can't thank my parents enough for not hovering over me in some bizarre helicopter-style parenting method. All my schoolfriends were raised in a similar way and we were, for the most part, gifted an independence and resilience that I for one am incredibly grateful for.

Nearing the end of today's gentle meander, at almost 11km, there was a famous crossing over the Barranco Sorabil river. By famous I mean there are heaps of photos and videos of it online. Not much more than a small stream for us, the landscape and the downstream attest to it being a much bigger deal if there is heavy rain or after a snow fall. I imagine the place could be a raging torrent and in that case you'd have to cross using the elevated roadway, but for us it was a simple matter of stepping across the dozen or so stone blocks. The last stretch into our destination saw one last climb up a hill and then we were done. A much-needed short day.

Popper and Paddy stopped in an albergue (Camino Hostel) where they were told they could have a pilgrim dinner with the rest of the folk in the place, but it was only for those staying there. I was booked a stone's throw round the corner in Casa Batit. It's a guest house above a family home with a bedroom, private bathroom and access to a shared lounge and kitchen. Clean, comfortable, equipped with a coffee filter machine. The TV didn't work but I doubt my Spanish would have been up to it.

After a shower, handwashing today's kit, and dressing in what I would wear for the walk tomorrow, minus socks and boots, I set off in my sandals and took a short walk back up the last hill into the village. I passed a group of kids playing ball on the street, and a few rough-looking chickens and dogs who were either guarding the kids, or waiting to be tormented by them. I couldn't work out which.

The last building on the right was a combination bar, restaurant, hotel and supermarket, but you may need to readjust your internal vision of it. I'm fairly sure it was a house built into the hillside with a small, covered seating area out front that accommodated about half a dozen glass-topped tables. To one side was a man, about my age, smoking.

I said, "Hola."

He answered the same and nodded towards the door.

I stepped into a narrow inside space with a bar counter about three metres long running along the left-hand side, some hot food cabinets on top of it, a tiny kitchen visible behind it and a vending machine leaning against it. Four dark wood tables sat empty in the open floorspace to the right.

Once they'd given me a glance, and figured I was just another 'pilgrim', all the customers sitting or standing at the bar, (six older men, rugged looking, lined faces and thinning hair) returned their attention to the small TV screen set high up on the wall at the end of the room.

I said, "Hola."

They said nothing.

The young man behind the bar greeted me in English. Of course he did. I ordered a baguette sandwich of cheese and ham which was outrageously good. Then I ordered what was going to become my drink of choice on the Camino, black tea with milk, and even though I don't usually, a spoonful of sugar.

He served me happily enough whilst also keeping one eye on the TV. On it was a sport I recognised as handball. Two competitors in a court the like of which I had only ever seen in my old high school, which had two of them, purpose built. They're like squash courts, but the one on the TV had a side missing and a grandstand packed full of spectators 'looking in' to the action on the court.

I 'oohed' as the player in red hit a great shot.

"You know balonmano?" the barman asked.

"I know handball, we played it at school," I said. "This seems the same?"

"This is Basque handball. A speciality of Basque pelota."

"Must be a big sport, lots of spectators."

"Massive, and the player in red, he is from here. I went to school with him. This is huge for us. Usually, the top players all come from Pamplona, but he is one of ours. Where did you play?"

I told him I came from Northern Ireland but I'd only ever seen this type of 'court handball' at my high school and I never saw any other courts, nor knew of anyone else who played it, outside of our school. To be honest, I had no idea why St Comgalls had two handball courts. I do know they were excellent for sneaking behind to have an illicit cigarette back in the day. What the connection between the Basque Country and Northern Ireland was that warranted the courts being built remained a mystery. Of course, I contemplated on how there were a lot more 'significant' areas of overlap between the Basque people and Northern Ireland's recent past, but I elected to steer clear of that topic. Old histories, recent histories, in fact, any histories are conversations you don't have with Northern Irish folk you just met, and I surmised you didn't have them here either.

As I was internally congratulating myself on being culturally aware, the man I had passed in the outside area came in. I greeted him in Euskara, the Basque language.

He frowned at me and walked on.

The young barman grinned. "You speak Euskara?"

"I don't know about speaking it. I can muster hello, thank you, good morning, please and goodbye. Oh and, how much is this? But obviously my pronunciation is awful," I said nodding towards the back of the man making his way to the toilet.

The younger man laughed. "Your pronunciation was okay. But most people of his generation don't speak it. My generation, we learnt at school, but his and older were…" he trailed off. "They didn't learn it."

I knew why. General Franco and the regime he oversaw had suppressed the Basque language and culture for decades. Yet it survived, and the language (and culture) is thriving, but a generation or more were lost to it in the mainstream. However, that was also a singular topic of conversation one didn't raise in this bar or anywhere else in Spain.

Rather, we chatted about Unai Laso, the local-born balonmano player, sport in general, football in particular, why I was doing the Camino and of course, what the weather was going to be like tomorrow. Our conversation strayed into a mix of sentences that fused into a crazy SpanglishEusk mix. It was fun trying to keep up with him, fluent as he was in all three, and I learnt a few more words of Euskara.

After an hour or so I bade farewell to the barman and went the few yards down the hill to my bed. The kids had gone inside their homes and the chickens had gone to roost. The dogs stood guard and snarled between bared teeth as I walked past, but that's all they did. A show of aggression, to keep any impromptu thief, or passing pilgrim, moving onwards.

On reflection, today had been a good idea. A couple of short hikes following the exertions of the mountains was exactly what we needed. It was enough to keep everything moving but also a solution to the fatigue levels of that first day. Could we have kept going today? Yes. Did we have to? Nope.

I got back to my room, made sure my kit was ready for tomorrow and turned in at 9:30pm.

Steps walked: 21,758 steps
Camino distance travelled: 11.66kms
Total elevation ascents: 228m
Total descents: 403m

Day 3

April 8th 2024
Viscarret-Guerendiáin - Zubiri
Planned distance: 11km
Planned steps: About the same as yesterday

Up early, but no need to bolt out the door. This was another 'short day' so we'd arranged to set off at around 8:30. I got myself gathered and wandered the thirty metres or so to the front of P&P's albergue, where I found a bar serving breakfast. A few small tables under a white marquee served as the 'restaurant' and a tiny side door led into a shop counter where a smiling lady charged me a handful of euros for some tea and toast with strawberry jam. Some half dozen other pilgrims sat at the chairs already, a couple of women from South America, a couple of men from Italy, another couple from Scandinavia. It was still early'ish and we had the good decency to keep the talk down to, "Hola. Where are you from? Buen Camino." Ah, the joys of mixing with fellow non-morning types.

Once P&P, perhaps I should refer to them as P-squared (P^2) from now on, anyway, once we'd caught up we set off on what was to be our second recovery day. Only 10.25km, most of it downhill apart from an early uphill stretch described in one of the guides as:

A demanding section rising 120 metres in under 1.5km.

If I meet the writer of that I may suggest an edit:

Lean a novel up against a wall, with about a thumb's width gap at the bottom and you have the angle of the rise out of Lintzoain. It goes on for 1.4kms. Have fun.

Not to over exaggerate, but if I were to post the elevation chart for that stretch, it is a line going up at an angle of 45 degrees. It was a killer on the calves. The rest of the day was a bimble in the park, almost. A few hills, but mostly flat and as we were still averaging around 800m elevation, stunning views over the most wonderful landscapes of pasture, rivers, wildflowers and far away mountains. That elevation was the reason the rest of the day was an, 'almost'. At some point, we had to drop down to 528m to get into the town of Zubiri and the guidebooks didn't mince their words. The path would be precarious. Even worse in the rain. Thankfully, our day was 14°C of balmy sunshine with hardly a cloud in the sky.

At a small rest stop before the hill to Zubiri, where a local entrepreneur has a food truck selling everything weary travellers might want, from hot toasted sandwiches to ice creams, we met Clara.

Ah! Did you ever meet someone and think, how marvellous? With her permission, Clara is allowing me to tell you that she is 71, hails from Alaska and is on her 6th Camino. I think this delightful force of nature can best be summed up when she said, "Yeah we have bears come near sometimes in Alaska. One ripped the door off my cabin once. That was a bit inconvenient." Clara was accompanied by her niece and the two of them were a riot of laughs and good humour. We'd meet up on a number of occasions over the next few days and they were always a delight, always smiling, always positive.

Once rested, we set off. Only to come back and grab Paddy's stick again, which was just as well, as he'd need it. The descent into Zubiri is not to be underestimated. The guidebooks had it right with the word *precarious*. It descends almost 300m over a 1-2km distance made up entirely of broken rock, shale and loose granite. I have no clue how you make it down safely in the rain. We were fortunate it remained dry. I was also fortunate in that I spent those last 2km into Zubiri in conversation with a guy from Bristol (I forgot to ask if I could use his name, so he'll have to stay anonymous).

Given the ankle-breaking nature of the track we spent about 30 minutes making our way down and that allowed us to have such a great talk about life, motivation, fitness, inspiration, journeys and ambition. At Zubiri he meandered on. I hoped we might cross paths again. We didn't. It didn't matter. He and I walked the descent into Zubiri and shared a moment of time. The conversation was great, the craic mighty as one might say. I tucked it away as another day being delightfully surprised by the Camino.

During about 6 hours, I had met Swedes, Italians, US Alaska, US California, UK English, a Northern Irish guy, Italians, French, two Argentinians and some Japanese. What a wonderful mix of humanity wandering along an ancient highway.

Zubiri was our stop for the night, but we'd arrived too early for our accommodation to let us in. Once again, P^2 were staying in an albergue, whilst I was in the budget cost, but not budget amenities, Txantxorena Hotel. After a few beers at one of the local bars, I got access to my room at about 2pm. It was worth the wait. A stunning, stone-floored, wooden ceiling room with a small balcony looking over fields that were home to a few horses. Clean, spacious, equipped with all you could want. I dropped my bag, sorted my kit, had a shower and wandered off to meet the lads. We needed to find a pharmacy for electrolytes (yeah, the Basque Chicken was still doing its thing, although a lot less than it had been) and Popper needed an insole for his boot. Then we did a quick tour of the town. It's stretched out in linear formation against the western bank of the Rio Arga. As a municipality, I think it's best described as functional. The river is beautiful. The old bridge is a striking combination of both. As we meandered, a light drizzle began to fall. It made the pavements slippy. Lord alone knows what it made the hill into the town like.

Hostels, hotels and restaurants abounded in Zubiri. We hadn't gone too far before finding the *El Palo del Avellano*, interestingly, an albergue none of us were staying in, but who welcomed all warmly. The cost of the meal was €17 per head, and for that you got salad, bread, soup, fish or meat main course and a choice of one of four desserts, plus a seemingly bottomless carafe of wine, as well as water.

I had a flaky, delicious cod, followed by a tiramisu that even the Italian at the table was impressed by. And the food wasn't the best part of the evening. The company was. For as well as the Italian, a further three, 'random' pilgrims joined us. Another smorgasbord of humanity, interesting stories, engaging ways and considerate manners. Paddy, Popper and I enjoyed their company immensely. Sadly, there were two more pilgrims at the table. There's the problem with karma and ying and yang. For every up, there is a down.

I shan't put his name, or that of his quieter travelling companion, but the boastful, loud, greedy and inconsiderate man did have a very distinctive Rat-tail hairstyle that lingers in my memory. I think it is more a reflection of my personality, rather than anything else, but as I can meet and take an instant liking to some folk, so I can meet and take an instant dislike to others. Paddy could see how uncomfortable Rat-tail was making me and did the only reasonable thing he could do, started laughing.

I did my best to block the rants and boasts coming from one side and, as is ying and yang, concentrated on the much more interesting conversations on the other. One of the men at the table was Ignazio, and his calming manner and happy, optimistic outlook on life did an amazing job at resetting the atmosphere of the space.

With the meal finished we said our farewells and wished each other, yes even RT, a Buen Camino!

Steps walked: 20,962 steps (A lot around the small town)
Camino distance travelled: 10.25kms
Total elevation ascents: 251m
Total descents: 499m

Day 4

April 9th 2024
Zubiri - Pamplona
Planned distance: 21km
Weather forecast: Rain, lots of it.

Waking early, but not as early as previous days, so my time zones were finally adjusting, I joined the other guests in the Txantxorena Hotel for a breakfast buffet that was varied and generous. An older couple from Canada, a younger couple from the UK, and two mates, Keith and John, also from the UK. These last two were on their umpteenth walking holiday together. This was their hobby and they'd done treks as varied as Hadrian's Wall in England and Everest Base Camp in Nepal. We talked about our respective first days, they'd been up on the Pyrenees on Sunday, so had missed the roughest of the winds, and we spoke about the descent into Zubiri yesterday. As we were preparing to leave, I noticed they had extremely small backpacks. What I would have called daypacks.

"Wow, you guys travel light."

"Yeah. Are you carrying that?" Keith asked, pointing to my pack.

"Uh, yeah, I though 7.5kg was good going, but what are they weighing in at, 2kg?"

They looked at me quizzically. "These are just for today; our main packs go ahead. Don't you send yours?"

I knew they were referring to the *Burro* companies that operate along all the Caminos. A service where, for €6 someone will pick up your bag and transport it to your next accommodation. Nowadays, not by donkey, but by car and van, although the idea for it stemmed from the luggage carrying donkeys or horses used in bygone days. To be honest, I wasn't that comfortable with the idea. I figured it might be, somehow, cheating, but neither did I want to be rude.

"And you do this every day?"

"Yeah," Keith said. "Why wouldn't you? We sure as heck didn't cart our own gear up to Everest Base Camp. We took what we needed and the rest was 'Sherpa'd' up there. This whole walking thing is meant to be enjoyable. It's a hobby. Why make it hurt more than you need to?"

I think I mustered an awkward smile, shrug of the shoulders and wished them well on their progress. They clapped me on the back and went off.

I walked around the corner to meet P² outside their albergue. Whilst waiting, I chatted to a young, mid-to-late 20s couple. The man, seeing the Australian flag on my shoulder, asked, "Aussie?"

"Yeah, you?"

"Israel," he said and I caught them share a look, perhaps not sure if saying their nation of birth was going to be a problem.

The news out of their homeland, regards the continuing conflict in Gaza, was bleak, and I wondered how they were coping. It's not easy being away from home when that home is rocked by violence, regardless of whatever 'side' of a divide one might be on. Neither though is it an easy conversation to be had with strangers.

"Shalom," I said.

They smiled gently and responded in kind.

"Originally I'm from Northern Ireland. Near Belfast." I added and paused a beat. "You guys doing okay? On your walk. In general?"

He looked at me, his head slightly tilted, contemplating. A tight smile and a nod.

"Your families okay?"

"Yes, thank you," they said in unison.

"That's all that matters," I said.

Another smile. And that was enough.

He returned to pulling on a bizarre pair of socks with individual toes in them. I'd seen them in trekking shops, but never for real.

"Do they work?"

"Yeah, I like them. But my sandals didn't do so well," he said, pointing to a blister. "But it will be fine. You just have to keep moving forward." They stood, wished me a Buen Camino and went on their way.

I reflected that sometimes, for example in a doorway in Zubiri on a Camino originally meant for Christian pilgrimage, a shared experience overrides cultures, religions and nationalities. The insanity of geopolitics and international affairs would do well to come for a walk.

I was stirred from my thoughts when Paddy appeared. He looked the complete opposite of well-rested. Popper following close behind looked shattered.

"You okay?"

"Not really," Paddy said.

As we set off, the story unfolded that in their small albergue room of about 12 beds, some people had been kept awake by the snores of others. When one 'snoree' had woken, and others had finally dropped off, one of the sleepers started to snore, reawakening all the others. Like a hellish baton-passing relay race of nasal reverberation. I shall not name names as to who was (or were) the culprits, but as Paddy, almost crying with laughter said, "I woke up once to see a little old Korean lady sitting up in bed almost weeping."

I did wonder if it was the same little old lady I'd almost thrown up on in the Pyrenees, but instead asked, "What about the earplugs you brought along?"

"You'd have needed industrial glue poured in to make a difference," Popper added. "C'mon, let's get as far away as we can."

"How was your night, Ian?" Paddy asked.

"Great. Warm shower, soft bed, good breakfast, quiet," I said with a wink, making sure to be out of arm's reach. "Did you at least get a good shower?"

"No comment." Popper said.

"And we need to stop for breakfast," said Paddy.

Later, at the first stop of the day, and between bites of a breakfast baguette, Popper asked, "How much did you pay for last night?"

"About 60 euros. You guys?"

"Thirty-two."

"Where are you staying tonight?"

"In an apartment in Pamplona."

"Can you get us into one?"

"Sure."

In my native Ulster parlance, the rest of the day was a bit 'dreeky'. Overcast, colder, drizzle turning to rain, back to drizzle and then when the precipitation stopped, a wet, clingy wind that soaked clothes and sought out fingers, noses and in my case today, bare knees. The long hiking trousers weren't working through the ups and downs of a Spanish spring's temperature fluctuations, so shorts were proving better, but at the price of cold knees. Ah well. It did make me consider that the trousers, cold weather gloves, fingerless gloves, beanie hat and ultra-thin merino-wool jumper I was carrying were unlikely to be used. So far every stop overnight had been in cosy accommodation and even when we were being blown away on the mountains, it hadn't been that cold. The average temperature was still in the teens of Celsius and the forecast for the next three weeks was 16-24°C and sunny days. The three of us concluded that we probably had a small box of gear that we could easily get rid of by using the Pilgrim Paq service of *Correos*, the Spanish postal system. For a minimal fee they will ship a box off to Santiago. I had looked it up and the destination sorting office was right beside the hotel we'd be staying in. Seemed like a no-brainer.

The terrain on this dreeky day was best described as up and down. In between the muddy up paths and muddier down paths, we tracked the flow of the Rio Arga. At one point almost able to step into the torrid waters flowing within inches of the path and at other times looking down on the broad current from maybe 150 feet high.

Yet despite the colder temperatures and the rain, the Camino continued to delight. From rosebuds to flowers I couldn't identify (but someone told me later they were magnolias) lining our route, to meeting with strangers, who because of overlaps and rest stops become temporary conversationalists. Like Anushka and Denise, two sisters from Oregon who stopped to admire the same weir as us. We passed three times and bumped into one another again in the city at the end of the day.

Or Clare Bridget, who lives in NZ, but who was a Baltimore, USA native. We spoke of many things, including the Baltimore bridge, which had recently collapsed after being struck by a ship, before she schooled all three of us (young men, in her guise) about the regular application of lip balm (SPF version). It was like your Mum telling you off ever so very politely. Then, with a smile, she was off again on her solitary Camino. Oh, I shouldn't forget to mention that Clare 'Bridget' gave me her middle name because she said her Dad was 4th generation US but was more Irish than the Irish, and so she was to be Bridget after our female 'Patron Saint'.

After 20+kms of a relatively grey day, we made the ancient city of Pamplona. It's been a settlement for over 2000 years, is the capital of Navarra, famous home to the Bull Running, immortalised by Hemingway, and as we passed by the closed Bull Ring, quickly identified as a city where, if not the majority then a sizeable few, want their independence from Spain or much greater autonomy at least.

I don't know enough about Basque politics and even if I did, this book is not the place to discuss them, but having people in a region within a country (regardless of which side they adhere to) who are unsettled, unnerved and unhappy is something my two walking companions and I can attest to as not making for the best of times. I imagined the young Israeli couple I had met that morning might also hold that opinion. I only hope in the Basque Country political movements continue to be the principal focus in the future. A return to the past would be a disaster.

Accommodation for all three of us was now going to be the Pozo Blanco Apartments. Kitchen, lounge, bathroom, bedrooms. My shower was so powerful I almost considered turning the water flow down a little, before reflecting that a long, hot, powerful shower is a just reward for twenty kilometres. I gave a little salute to the shower designers and plumbers of Navarra.

Once sorted for tomorrow, I went out to find the Office of Tourism, as our apartments didn't have a Camino 'stamp' and I knew you could get one done in the tourist place. By the time I got there, it was shut. But I did bump into Clara and her niece again, so that was an unlooked-for bonus.

This was my first experience of meeting people on the Camino who, although we'd only spent half an hour in conversation two days before hand, felt like they were familiar friends. I didn't think of it as we chatted, but as we went our separate ways it struck me as a curious mix of making complete sense, whilst also being a bit weird. It's not like you do that type of thing in the real world. Meet someone, have a brief chat, then meet them later and feel an immediate sense of fellowship. I think that was when I figured out how the rest of this book would be structured.

On my way back to the apartment, I stopped at a Coviran (a chain of supermarkets) stocked up on some items for tomorrow and discovered the supermarket's own brand of soft fruit candies called Covinolas. More about them later!

In the early evening, Paddy and I headed out to find the nearest post office. The sun had come out and the streets of Pamplona were busy and colourful. The architecture in the plazas and boulevards, magnificent. Even the post office was located in a beautifully fronted building of classic style, yet the automated doors opened into a modern, sleek space. Taking an automated ticket, we waited our turn.

Eventually, Paddy and I moved forward, put the things we didn't need into a single box and paid €25 to have it whisked away to Santiago. Seemed like a great idea.

On reflection, it wasn't and after a decision we made a few days later, it was entirely unnecessary… Still, at the time it made sense.

Once done, we set out to find food. I had wanted to go and sit at the historic Café Iruña, in the main *Plaza del Castillo*, once more tracking Hemingway's steps and closing the circle on The Sun Also Rises, from Le Select in Paris to this fine café in Pamplona, but as the evening darkened, rain clouds swept in and the night became a bit wet and miserable. Instead of sitting alfresco in a café, we went to the Zanpa bar and restaurant. It was bright, warm and 'bunged' with locals. The food was excellent and when Paddy's dish of scallops appeared as baby squid the mistake was remedied in minutes. By the time we were heading back, Pamplona was into her second wind, and even on this nondescript Tuesday her bars and eateries were thronged. Had the temperature been warmer, the rain 'drier' and we three not in need of a good night's sleep, it would have been a fine place to partake in a nightcap (or two).

Our final stop was into a small shop called Caminoteca that sold all sorts of souvenirs, but crucially also stamped Pilgrim Passports. With that job done, we called it a night.

Steps walked: 40,344 (Which included wandering around Pamplona and set a new 'daily' personal best (PB) for me)
Camino distance travelled: 21.20kms
Total elevation ascents: 582m
Total descents: 647m

Day 5

April 10th 2024
Pamplona - Puente la Reina
Planned distance: 23km

The morning began with a self-cooked breakfast of poached eggs, toast, tea, coffee. We had kitchens, why not use them.

Once sorted we headed off at about 8:00am and I managed to lead the lads on a circuitous route through the main plaza and eventually onto the route proper. The Camino is, even in the mountains, fantastically well signposted with yellow arrows and shells, and in the cities, accompanying yellow and blue signs have 'CAMINO' written on them. I mean... you couldn't possibly take the wrong turn... could you?

Anyway, I had forgotten to start my Garmin watch tracker, so thankfully the loop we made is lost to posterity. And yes, for any ex-military, this is why you do not give an officer the map. I eventually clicked 'start' next to the appropriately named Plaza de Santiago and we were on our way to Puente la Reina, (Bridge of the Queen).

The queen in question being Muniadona of Castile, who reigned round these parts in the 1000's. She died in 1066 but left a superb example of a Romanesque bridge so pilgrims can keep their feet dry. I made a mental note to thank Her Majesty when going over the bridge tomorrow. For now, we found ourselves walking through the most idyllic of mornings.

A picture-book-blue sky, a bright warming sun and busy streets leading us to Pamplona's university area, full of enthusiastic looking students, who smiled and said Buen Camino as we traversed the parks and gardens. The happy, vibrant youngsters in stark contrast to the older members of their society. A fact that Paddy, Popper and I now became acutely aware of. The older generation in the Basque country were, let's be kind and say, reserved.

In 'small town' Northern Ireland, one can walk down any street and strangers will nod, say hello, or offer a, "How you doing?" It was the same even at the height of the Troubles. This friendly way can also be observed across large swathes of Ireland, Scotland, Wales and England, although it gets a lot less frequent in London. I mean, try striking up a conversation on the Tube. And yes, I realise these are huge, sweeping generalisations, but they are born out of huge, sweeping observations that I am sure many would concur with. It tends to be a more rural habit, yet since arriving in Spain, for the most part we'd been in rural areas and it was not the same.

To be fair, I hadn't really thought about it, as every host in every accommodation I'd stayed in couldn't have been more friendly, but 'outside' in the villages, the locals we had passed on streets or lane-ways had not offered a hello or a Buen Camino. They didn't even make eye contact but tended to look down and pass on by.

Yet these youngsters heading to their studies, were a different breed. Happy, enthused, engaging. It couldn't all be down to youthful optimism. I remembered back to the bar on that first night. The only person to greet me had been the younger barman. Aside from a per-functory nod from the smoker outside, the older men in the bar hadn't acknowledged me at all.

It was Popper who first mentioned it and Paddy and I were quick to agree. We had no answers, but we had a few theories. Perhaps the Basque people, having been a people apart for so long, were naturally insular and protective of their unique and truly ancient culture and language. Perhaps the youth, with easy access to social media, the Internet and their resultant 'shrinking world' were not. Perhaps the systematic repression of the area over generations had caused a mistrust of outsiders and because the younger people hadn't suffered through those times they weren't like that. Perhaps the older inhabitants were simply fed up with a bunch of overly privileged eejits calling themselves pilgrims wandering about the place. Perhaps the youngsters, not having been around as long, were still open to the whole idea.

Perhaps, perhaps, perhaps.

I do know one thing. Whilst thinking about stuff like this, you can get an awful lot of walking done. By 11:30am we had walked 11.5kms and were in Zariquiegui. There was a small shop, *Teinda el Peregrino*, the pilgrim shop, which was also a café and had toilets. A small tip, there are lots of cafes and shops along the way and most have toilets, but few have toilet paper. Take your own. And pocket soap. I used the Sea to Summit pocket soap wafers. Google them. Also, seems only fair that if using their facilities you should buy something, even if only a small bottle of water, or leave a few euros on the counter.

Across from Tienda el Peregrino was a church. As you already know, I'm not the religious type, but it looked old, and I like old, so I wandered over. The *Iglesia de San Andrés,* Church of Saint Andrew, had a Romanesque door portal and a gothic roof. It was built in the second half of the 12th century and substantially modified during the 1500s. The golden backdrop to the altar portrays St Andrew's cruci-fixion on an x-shaped cross as he said he wasn't worthy to die as Christ had. Hence the reason the St Andrew's cross, as on the flag of Scotland, is a Saltire, (an x-shaped cross). The cross of St Patrick, used as an Irish symbol, most notably within the Union flag of the United Kingdom, is also a Saltire, but the reasons for that are a de-bate that would take up another chapter on its own and thankfully, this ain't the place for that! As for this church, wow! Peaceful, calm, cool (in all senses of that word). I loved it. There was a local lady acting as volunteer guide and you could also get a specific stamp for your pilgrim passport. I figured it would do no harm.

Exiting back into the morning sun, pilgrims who we had passed earlier were gathering in this hamlet of Zariquiegui; resting, hydrating, checking feet and preparing for the next 2.5kms of the journey that would bring us up to the summit of *Alto del Perdón*, located in the *Sierra del Perdón* mountain range. It's named for a chapel that used to stand there, dedicated to Our Lady of Forgiveness but is much more famous now for the sculpture that sits atop it.

Variously referred to as *El Perdon*, or Monument of the Alto del Perdón or the Pilgrim Sculptures, whatever you call it, it's iconic. Made from sheet metal coloured to a deep rust-brown, it represents pilgrims across the ages, with horses, mules and a dog or two, making their way over the mountain. It also details the fluctuating fortunes of the pilgrimage itself, from the beginnings in the middle ages to the modern experience. The artist, Vicente Galbete has managed to invoke a sense of the wind gusting around by making the pilgrims lean into their progress. Installed back in 1996, it provides an obvious photo opportunity, but don't forget to look past it to the most awe-inspiring panoramic views of Navarra. If you want to know more about the meaning behind each of the figures, then Google: Jean Mitchell-Lanham, *The Lore of the Camino de Santiago*.

To get up to your photo op, you have to climb the hill. It's also got a meaning for the more faithful and the English translation of its name is The Hill of Forgiveness. Pilgrims are meant to forgive others or ask for personal forgiveness with each step. For the less faithful amongst us it is still a tough climb, regardless of the penance you are undergoing, or not.

I started it in the company of Paddy, then Popper and then a French lady, (again, didn't ask her permission, so we shall call her Gabriella) who was also in a loose walking formation with her friends. We chatted in Frenglish, our conversation ranging from grandchildren and holidays to the places we'd lived and careers we'd enjoyed. The flowers on the rough path were beautiful, but the broken surfaces over some larger gaps, spanned by teetering rocks, made the climb a challenge. I was grateful for having trekking poles.

Depending on what source you believe, the hill is 770m or 1039m. My knees and thighs reckoned it was the higher of those two. My Garmin figured it at 764m. I suspect the Garmin is correct.

After about 45 minutes, Gabriella and I made the summit and caught up with our respective friends. About twenty or so pilgrims had made the top together. As the earlier arrivals departed, so a trickle of others joined. Everyone took turns to get their photo next to the sculpture and the small groups of strangers that found themselves in proximity chatted about the climb, the use of trekking poles or sticks, the Pyrenees, the albergue experience, the food and all manner of stuff that was now our stock-in-trade small talk.

Away from the main sculpture, on the other side of the road is, to my mind, a much more moving piece of artwork. A monument to those from the area that were killed during the Spanish Civil War. It is worth a moment of reflection. I thought of the many Irish who had fought in the International Brigades, and those, drawn by whatever reasons they held, who had decided to fight on the other side. As I was reading the monument's information board, some women were chatting nearby, their accents lifted on the blustery wind.

Four friends from Dublin, doing another section of the Camino, parts of which they had done last year and the remainder they'd do in other years to come. I'd not considered you could do it in bits. It seemed such a sensible approach.

The seven of us, in loose discussion, set off down the hill and were soon faced with another brutal stretch of track. It's not as long as the descent into Zubiri but it was rougher in places. At one point, as I put my right trekking pole down onto what looked like solid ground and took a step, the solid ground turned out to be a pocket of sand-covered shale. It went one way and I went down onto both knees. My left one smacked down about an inch away from a spiked boulder. One of the Dublin ladies gave a small gasp. "Are you okay?"

"Aye."

"Are you sure?" She reached out a hand.

I decided the poles were probably an easier way and used them to leverage myself back up. There was no blood, nor bruising on my wee knees, no pain or ricks or cricks elsewhere. I'd fallen onto the only flat piece of sandy soil in sight. Lucky me. Onwards.

Once off the hill, the remainder of the day was on flatter ground with wide blue skies and a strong sun. I was thankful for my hat, for the 'Buff' I wore around my neck and for the sunscreen in my kit.

Villages and rest stops abounded on this section and pilgrims, strung out along the way, would gather up at these, like leaves caught in a gentle eddy. Twirling around and chatting. The Dubliners, a few Americans, the French friends, quite a few Spanish, and a myriad more. My favourite quote of the day was from Roger from southern California.

"What made you do the Camino, Roger?"

"My wife, Teri," he said turning to the lady next to him.

Can't argue with that for a reason. Our paths crossed most of the day with Teri and Roger. Retired, vibrant, eloquent and interesting people who made every encounter engaging.

Our last stop, before Puente la Reina, and where, once again, we all bunched up, was in Uterga at the impressive *Camino Del Perdón Albergue-Restaurante*. A pleasant alfresco area to its front, great bar, excellent food, good beer. Even though we sat longer than we should have, it was worth it for the craic. Although dropping my phone on to the concrete as I was swinging my backpack up was not an ideal thing to do. Thank goodness for the screen protector that took the hit rather than the screen.

The final 5km, probably due to the sun and the beer, definitely seemed much, much longer than the first 5km of the day. That became another trait we noticed as the days went on. Afternoon kilometres were longer and harder than morning ones. Yet the bottom line was always the same: you simply keep putting one foot in front of the other, and eventually you would get there. So… we did just that.

At one point, when it seemed the destination might never appear and we three were flagging a little, I produced the pack of Covinolas. They are mere soft fruit candies, but at times like this they were a Godsend. Over the next few days, come the mid-afternoon slump, Paddy and Popper would find me. The rest of our loose company of familiar faces also looked forward to 'Covinolas Time' although when Popper called out a little too loudly, "Hey mister? Got any of them there sweeties?" we got a very strange look from some unfamiliar passing pilgrims who quickened their pace and hurried away!

Arriving, finally, into Puente la Reina, P² were glad to find their hotel was the first building they came to. I was in a small place tucked away at the heart of the old town. We figured we'd catch up for dinner. As it was, we didn't, but we did WhatsApp quite a bit. Mainly due to an encounter I had on the inner fringes of the town.

Slogging in after 20+kms on a day that had turned out to be warm, Keith and John (from back in Zubiri) were sitting relaxed and unflustered having a beer.

"Still got the backpack?" Keith commented.

"Yeah," I smiled, pulling up to have a chat.

"You said you were ex-military?" John asked.

"Yeah."

"You had to carry all your kit so you had it with you, didn't you?"

"Yep," I agreed, then added, "But I rarely did this type of long route march."

"Yeah, but I'm just saying, you don't need to do that anymore. You can send it ahead, it will be waiting for you. Suppose you think it's some form of cheating?"

"Kind of," I agreed.

"Well, consider this," Keith added. "You can also do the Camino barefoot you know?"

"I've heard of some that do it like that, yeah," I said.

"Would you?"

"Of course not."

"No," said Keith. "You wear boots to make it a bit easier, more enjoyable?"

John smiled at his mate's analogy and added, "Likewise, you can also send you kit forward. It's just a thought."

I bade them farewell and by the time I had found my jewel of a hotel, I'd contacted the lads. Both Paddy and Popper agreed that it wasn't the dumbest idea they'd ever heard.

They'd book some accommodation in advance for tomorrow and have their bags lifted. I agreed. Only problem was I didn't have a daypack and Puente la Reina didn't have a camping shop, or at least one I could find. It was fine. I'd cope for a day and get one in Estella tomorrow.

Diane, the lady at the front desk of my hotel, couldn't have been more helpful. She gave me an envelope for the courier service called *Jaco Trans* and said she'd sort out the pick-up. All I had to do was put €6 in the envelope, write the address of where I would be staying, attach it to my bag and make sure it was in reception by 7.00am.

In fact, she made it too easy and I was lulled into not reading the envelope. Apparently, each Jaco Trans service was split into zones covering separate districts, but all of them had the requirement for the customer to contact them and let them know about pick-ups and drop-offs. Due to Diane being so helpful, I mistakenly thought each hotel or accommodation would do it for us. I'd learn in a few days' time that no, that was not the case. But for now, all was good.

A word about the *Hotel El Cerco*. It's down a small side street and was a fortunate find. Booked using the same criteria as before, the single room was tiny but incredibly functional, clean and warm. Like a luxury ensuite monk's cell! Tiled floor, exposed brickwork, wooden shuttered window and another shower that was a testament to the plumbers of Navarra.

Kit sorted, me sorted, I wandered out to find something to eat. Instead, I found a small supermarket with a display board outside advertising Lemon Meringue Cornetto Ice Creams. Well… you would have bought one too… wouldn't you?

Ice cream in hand, I wandered down to the river's edge to get a look at the bridge that gave the town its name. Four young women were sitting on the riverbank chatting. I wandered past them, savouring an ice cream flavour that I'd pay good money to have imported into Australia. Honestly, it was superb!

As I was turning to leave, one of the women, who had been sketching in a small notebook, pointed to the ice cream.

"Is it nice?"

"Yes, very. Lemon Meringue Cornetto. Thought it would make a wonderful dessert."

"Oh, that does sound good. What did you have for dinner?"

"Ah well… You see…"

I gave a fake hurrumph of a cough and put on my best 'stern' accent. "As I am lots older than all of you, I suggest you do as I say, not as I do. You should have your dinner first before ice creams."

Thankfully they got the humour.

"You're Northen Irish," the artist asked quizzically, looking at the Australian flag on my sleeve.

"Yeah."

And so, a conversation ensued about who we all were, where we all came from and why we were all here.

"Why did you go to Australia?"

I recounted the potted history of meeting my wife, how we ended up living where we do. Part of that story involves the use of a very early version of email and deciding to get married after three weeks. Twenty-six years ago. They were amazed. Probably more so that someone my age was able to use the Internet, but they were polite enough not to say that. In turn they told their stories.

Serena, from Surrey, living on the Southbank of London, near to The Globe, artist, comedian, fluent in Spanish. The Camino was a thing she always wanted to do and so here she is, doing it. Along with a loose collection of acquaintances that she meets up with after a day of walking. Sometimes she walks with them, sometimes with others, sometimes alone.

Turned out the other three women were not part of 'Serena's cohort' and all four had simply met at the riverbank this evening.

Bethany, in her early twenties, on a sabbatical from studies having majored in neuroscience and Spanish. The Camino was on her wish list, so here she was, travelling solo and happy with how it was all going so far. Her home was Kentucky.

"Have you ever been to Kentucky?" she asked.

"Sadly, no. I would like to, especially as it's home to the Derby and the Maker's Mark Bourbon distillery."

She laughed. "Yep, that's us. Bourbon and horses. I don't like the taste of the first and I'm allergic to the second. I'm a real Kentucky girl!"

There's was a French joke to be made about how it would be worse if it was the other way round, but I passed on it.

Lucy, from Ohio, also in her twenties, also travelling solo and also fulfilling a wish list of doing the Camino.[2]

And Julie. From Germany. An environmental science graduate as well as being a dancer and a yoga practitioner. Doing the Camino for the headspace and the mindfulness. She walked with a hula hoop in her kit and on occasions over the next few days, we'd pass her as she took time out to stand barefoot, grounding herself and somehow generating a calmness that was infectious.

They spoke at length about their schooldays, their universities, the studies they had completed and the future ones they might do. Their hopes and ambitions, and their experiences on the Way. They all agreed that they felt safe walking the Camino Francés on their own.

As the sun began to dip and mossies began to appear, I bade them a goodnight and went in search of the main course I should have had

---

[2] Sadly, Lucy got injured a couple of days after this and had to withdraw at the halfway point to Santiago. She has plans to return and finish it someday.

earlier. The choice of restaurant was limited and I elected to go with Bar Aloa.

Now to be clear, this book, in so much as it is a guide, will try not to be negative about anyone or anything. If I don't mention a certain hotel or restaurant, it's because I think that the old adage of, "If you can't say something nice, don't say anything," is a worthwhile touchstone... for the most part.

However, if the service is so bad or the food so mediocre as to warrant it, then I will comment. Bar Aloa was one of those.

They served their version of a pilgrim menu. Widespread on the Camino, this is a three-course meal with wine for about 10-20 euros depending on where you are. The meal in Zubiri had been one such offering. We'd had similar on a couple of occasions since. You may think for that amount of money it would necessarily be mediocre, but far from it. To be honest, it was usually too much food for me. Imagine a large plate of Spaghetti Bolognese as a starter (First Plate), followed by a fish or meat dish with tons of vegetables (Second Plate), followed by a dessert.

The Bar Aloa restaurant, about eight tables in a room to the rear of the long narrow bar area, was half full. One table taken up by 'The Dubliners' who were just finishing and leaving as I arrived. A couple more tables were hosting other pilgrims that I'd seen, but not talked to, on the road.

The pilgrim menu was fairly standard, but I didn't want a three-course meal. When the waiter thrust a paper 'dinner mat' in front of me I asked, in Spanish, if I could have the starter. Only the starter. The waiter looked at me like I'd killed his pet dog.

I thought perhaps I had misspoken. I tapped the translator app and got it to ask in Spanish. It said what I had said. I was pleased. The waiter looked even more upset. He mumbled something and sodded off.

A woman appeared. "What do you want?' she asked in English.

"May I just have the starter, please?" I asked, pointing to the menu. "I'm happy to pay the standard price, but I only want the starter."

"Wine?"

I was tempted to groan in a strangulated voice, but figured that my humour would not go over well, so I said, "Yes please."

I got a single tut in response.

The food was tasteless, the wine as rough as the feet that trod it. The service bordered on aggressive. I finished, put the money on the table and left. Perhaps I caught them on a bad day. Perhaps.

To console myself, I passed the small supermarket again and stopped to buy more Covinolas. As I left the premises I found that, somehow, I had managed to buy another Cornetto as well. It helped me sleep.

Steps walked: 41,043 (Another PB, quite a bit of it wandering round Puente la Reina)
Camino distance travelled: 24.08kms
Total elevation ascents: 575m
Total descents: 660m

A postscript for this day.

As I was walking back to my digs, I met Anna, the lady from Quebec who had set out from StJPdP on the same day as us. Her arm was in a sling. She had arrived into Pamplona last night, and like us had been greeted by rain. She slipped going in the door to her accommodation. Reaching out to steady herself, the door opened, her hand caught and she ripped her shoulder. Unable to zip up, let alone carry, a backpack, she had struggled on for today but was now, sadly, calling it quits. Returning home to Canada in the next few days, she was determined to come back and complete her Way. We parted and she bade me farewell with a poignant, "Buen Camino."

Day 6

April 11th 2024
Puente la Reina - Estella
Planned distance: 22km

Six days in and my favourite one so far. It began with a small, light breakfast in the small, light breakfast room of the Hotel El Cerco, as I watched my bag being picked up and whisked away. Well, almost. They picked it up and then queried the apartment address that I'd be staying in. They couldn't drop it inside a private apartment building so they'd have to drop it at the Estella municipal albergue, about a two-minute walk from the apartment, "Was that okay?"

"Sure!"

As I watched it depart, I did consider that if this was to be the way of things, then sending all that kit forward to Santiago in two separate consignments had been a waste of time, but you live and learn.

By 8am the three of us had met up again and started the day by walking over Her Majesty Queen Muniadona's gift to pilgrims. The high point atop the central arch of the six-arched Romanesque 11th century bridge gifts great views of the Rio Arga and the valley to north and south. I remembered to say a thank you. I then said a lot of other things under my breath as we toiled up an almost 150m rise that left the Arga valley behind (and below) us.

That 1000-year-old bridge would be usurped later in the day by a Roman cobbled road and the *Puente Romano,* a Roman Bridge, near to Cirauqui. Two millennia beats a mere one. Except... on investigation, recent archaeology has suggested that the road was a medieval construct (as was the bridge) based on styles that the Romans used in Spain, but not here. There is scant evidence the Romans came this way at all, as no Roman artifacts have been found on the road to Estella. There were Roman roads that went through northern Spain, but further north. Ah well, never mind. I didn't know that at the time and was extremely happy to be making my way along what I thought were 2000-year-old pathways that real legionnaires had walked on.

Now, I don't want to be too 'out there' but Popper took some photos that day and one of them was of his shadow on an old stone wall. When, many months later, I was looking through all our photos to select some for this book, all I could see was the shadow of a Roman legionnaire. If you think I'm losing the plot, I'd completely understand, but I've included the photo in the images within the book. See what you think.

Back on the day itself, I crossed the 'Roman' bridge in the company of Ignazio, whom I'd first met at the Zubiri dinner. Born in Sicily, he lives in England, is a keen walker and an even keener yachtsman. As at the meal, so too on the road, he had an amiable, calming manner coupled with an optimistic, buoyant outlook. We walked and talked for a couple of hours and he recounted how, because of his work in neuroscience research and medical trials, he had opened a Camino inspired 'JustGiving' page for research into Motor Neurone Disease (MND). He'd already passed £4,000 and was humbled by how friends, family and complete strangers were contributing to a cause he felt deeply about.

Long stretches of today passed adjacent to vineyards in the valley of the Rio Arga, before leaving them behind and crossing broad vistas of rape seed, glinting yellow in a strong sun. The reassuring, soft tramp of pilgrims was accompanied by birds singing and the scents of freshly mown grass and wildflowers. Narrow pathways with poppies growing from the verges, dusty tracks and small villages kept the scenery ever changing, as did the company. Familiar faces passed or were passed and some new ones were encountered as we strode on towards Estella.

In Villatuerta, with about 7kms to go, sitting at a table on the narrow sidewalk out front of the Marta Café, we met Siegfried (from Devizes in Wiltshire), Jürgen (from Germany), Biretta (from the Netherlands) and Megan (from Canada - that part of Canada that sounds a wee bit Norn Irish). They looked like life was calm, unfettered and joyous. If they read this, I owe them a thank you as their enthusiasm and laughter were great to brush by on a sultry afternoon and their energy was contagious.

It was also good to agree with Jürgen (as we were both supporters of Liverpool Football Club) that he had a great name and that his namesake was a star, even if recent results were hard to take.

Once past 20km I did wonder where the destination had gotten itself to. Afternoon kilometre syndrome was kicking in, but this time it felt like the town itself was hiding. Usually, the end is enticingly close and the destination reveals itself, upon a hill or from across a plain, welcoming you with a taunt of, 'here I am, though I'm further than you think', but 150-metres from where my GPS-enabled gadgets said Estella should be, I still had seen no clue. Then, rounding a final bend and taking a rise in the road, the old town, with majestic churches, appeared like a Spanish, 'Brigadoon'. When it was needed.

I was in a 'medieval apartment' on the south side of the river Ega. A modern set of rooms within a medieval building. It was clean, had a well-appointed kitchen, a bathroom with very fancy taps, a good shower (where doesn't) and the biggest fireplace I'd ever seen in a rental. Ironically the place was a bit chilly. I wasn't going to try lighting a fire, I didn't have enough flammable material to fill the grate, so I kept my fleece on.

After I had retrieved my bag from the municipal albergue, which looked magnificent, I found my trusty little Scrubba clothesline was missing. I don't mean it had been taken. I mean in my excitement to get my bag downstairs in time to have it picked up that morning, I had left the clothesline hanging in the bathroom. My annoyance wasn't about the cost of it (which was about three bucks) but the fact I hadn't looked after my kit properly. Old habits and all that. I could hear my long-ago instructors in basic training yelling at me to check and check and check again before setting off.

Speaking of kit, P² and I met up and set off to find a shop that would sell daypacks. Sure enough, not far away, we found a camping shop called, S*alir del paso* which translates, most appropriately as, 'Get out of trouble'. They had daypacks for about €20 and the kind lady threw in a new washing line for me, gratis.

Continuing our wander around Estella we could have done with paying heed to the name of the shop a bit more, as we mistakenly meandered into what could best be described as the rough end of town.

I do realise that no one outside of my hometown is going to get this next reference, and maybe not even some who are from it, but if you're from Larne, and you are of a certain age, then picture the borderland of Craigyhill and Antiville, or the Antiville shops, or the Craigyhill ones, back in the early to mid-70s… the part of Estella we had found ourselves in was that sort of rough! Best I can explain for non-Larne-yins, is to imagine the dark end of a street. As you walk towards it, shadowy types appear out of shadowy places and look threateningly at you, envious of your straight teeth and ten fingers.

We walked on. Quickly. And found ourselves in the main plaza watching children organise their own football games using old arch-ways, jumpers and saplings for goalposts. Their delight as they ran unhindered and celebrated scoring like they were playing for Madrid or Barca was good for the soul.

We took an outside table at the *Restaurante Bar Florida*, next to a group of young men and women, including Serena. They chatted easily whilst she doodled, spectacularly, an image of the *Iglesia de San Juan Bautista*, the Church of Saint John the Baptist. The twin spired, triple-crossed church dominated the *Plaza de los Fueros* and its high mounted clock face caught the last rays of the setting sun. It's diffi-cult to translate Fueros, but charters, as in legal charters, comes close – sort of the town hall square I guess.

As for the food, the restaurant had a lot of shellfish, crab, lobster and other crustaceans, which was most definitely **not** for me. I was grateful to be sitting at an outside table that took most of the aromas aways on a breeze. They also had a pilgrim's menu that was even more substantial than most, yet intriguingly, at the foot of the page they also had listed, ham, eggs and chips. Turns out, far from it being an Irish or British stable food, it is also a local dish around here. I'm not kidding. *Huevos Estrellados.* It was great.

Steps walked: 36,032
Camino distance travelled: 23.16kms
Total elevation ascents: 781m
Total descents: 702m
(Yes, those stats are right, it was an up and down day)

Day 7

April 12th 2024
Estella – Los Arcos
Planned distance: 22km (again)

Up, packed, bag dropped at the municipal albergue, out into the cool morning of more blue skies and a gentle sun warming the day. It's early April. This is great! Who needed all that cold weather stuff?

Paddy, Popper and I met again on a bridge and made our way through the quiet streets of the old town, passing the formidable *Iglesia de San Miguel*, a 12th century church atop a rocky outcrop. It was imposing now, and I wondered what pilgrims in the middle ages had made of its grandeur. Exiting the town and joined by others leaving the various albergues, hotels and apartments, we prepared for the first 9km of today; a climb from 450m up to 687m.

Not long into our journey we stopped at *La Forja de Ayegui,* the Forge of Ayegui (Ayegui is the name of the municipality). There, Jesús Ángel Alcoz, a blacksmith and artisan metal worker has a work-ing forge, gallery and exhibition space open to view. The man himself was there at his anvil and looked up to say, "Hola."

I wasn't surprised that he was short and wiry, yet exuded strength from every pore. I never met my blacksmith grandfather but pictures show him to have had a similar stature. I was still reflecting on that when Jesús asked, "¿Hola?"

In broken Span-glish I managed to say, "Sorry. Yes, hello. I was thinking about my grandfather. He was a blacksmith. The last of a lineage going back for 300 years."

Jesús said he had learnt from his own father.

I bought a small piece of his work to carry with me. I'd later gift the hand-worked twisted metal cross to my wife. As I was leaving, Jesús gifted me a miniature fleur-de-lis. *"Por suerte."*

Walking on, it wasn't long until we reached the famous *Fuente del Vino*. A water fountain with two taps. One for water, one for wine. I had carried my collapsible cup for this very purpose. The wine is a long tradition for pilgrims and so I had a mouthful or two. Let's say, red wine at 10am is an acquired taste. I reverted to the water.

Lunch was in the small hamlet of Azqueta at the wonderful café bar *l'antorcha* (The Torch) run by Raymond from the Netherlands who had been a pilgrim last year, met a Spanish lady and now they run this cafe together. It also has a jukebox. A proper one! Raymond was a most genial host, and the tea and sandwiches were fantastic. Albeit that might have been due to the previous 7.5km being up, up and more up. There was another couple of Ks of ascending terrain to do and then we'd be into one of the first sections of this Camino route where there was little shade and little in the way of stops.

All the guidebooks advise to stock up on provisions, water especially, in Villamayor de Monjardín before setting out on this stretch. Now's as good a time as any to mention that there are numerous opportunities to buy water or other drinks (including beer) along the Camino Francés and there are also publicly provided and maintained 'potable' water fountains at many places. If a fountain's water is not drinkable, it says so in clear signs. Sometimes there are stretches where you have to carry more.

After the first 9kms up from Estella, the land now tracked downwards in a gentle ambling manner that offered broad vistas of rape fields and stunning deep-blue skies that were a joy to the eye and a boost to the wellbeing of the spirit. The remaining hills overlooked, rather than stood in the way of, the pilgrim's progress.

One of those hills, on the approach to Monjardín, has the *San Esteban de Deyo* also called the *Castillo de Monjardín*, sitting atop it. The ruined castle is at an elevation of 890 metres and some souls climb up to it on their Camino. We didn't. I was more than happy to gaze up and admire (imagine) the Roman foundations that underly it and have been repeatedly built on over centuries. The rest of the day was spent wandering through idyllic scenery in good company.

I spent much of the afternoon chatting to Doug. A quiet, big man who speaks softly. This is his second Camino and as he was telling me a story from his first, the intensity of the memory brought him to a stop. He had, a year or more ago, watched two men who had been on opposite sides in a complicated and bloody civil war, bond as friends on the Way. It had humbled him then. It caught him off guard now. Doug would be another whom we would meet off and on as we progressed. We all shared WhatsApp details and Paddy, Popper, him and I drop the occasional update even now. A message in late September 2024 told of his latest journey, walking in India.

I took a break at the height of the afternoon sun amidst an olive tree grove, to change socks and do a 'foot check'. Doug ambled on.

Later, arriving into Los Arcos, I found the Hostal Suetxe and, as their water was off for about an hour due to a small plumbing issue, I settled myself in a bar across the street and waited for Paddy and Popper. My watch said I had done 33,333 steps. I considered not moving for the rest of the day, but a shower and a meal were destined to win out. After a beer and an agreement to meet in town, I returned to my room; clean, functional (another great shower) and again with a wooden shuttered window that this time looked out onto a church and the hills beyond.

In the evening, visiting the small town's main plaza, I ran into Ignazio and some others who invited me to join them in the Mavi bar and restaurant. A quick message exchange revealed Paddy was having a kip, so I took them up on the kind offer. This time I opted for the full Pilgrim's Menu and for €15 had a superb three course meal, picking from one of five choices on each course, plus water and red wine. The food was good, but the mix of people at the table made the experience great. Two walking friends from Luxembourg, who I sadly didn't write the names of in my notes and at this distance cannot recall. Ignazio, Camille from France and Tim and Deb from Virginia. The conversation, in a multitude of languages, flowed effortlessly and the two Luxembourgers left me in awe. They swapped, almost mid-sentence, between Luxembourgish, French, and English. They also spoke fluent Spanish, German and Italian and could get by in a few others. Camille was fluent in a few and Ignazio could speak Italian as well as English. All of them kindly accommodated Tim, Deb and myself and mostly spoke in English.

This evening was the first time I properly encountered the Camino providing, other than gifting us a hiking supply shop when we'd needed to buy daypacks. Turns out Camille, an experienced hiker with ample time and distance spent in the Alps, so this wasn't her first 'rodeo', had, for inexplicable reasons, developed massive and severe blisters on her foot. She was, like the Dubliners, doing the Camino in stages and would be trekking from StJPdP to Burgos this time, but she had figured her Camino was over this morning. Then she'd met Tim and Deb. Tim is a retired Podiatric surgeon. An actual, bona fide, foot specialist. He treated Camille (as best you can when on a trail) and she continued walking.

Paddy and Popper joined us a little later and then we three headed to the adjacent bar for a nightcap. The only sad bit of news was that, at some point today, Paddy had left his stick behind at one of the stops. We gave a toast to the stick and trusted it would be found by someone in need of it, then called it a night. Outside, there was a statue that looked across to the children's playground, still abuzz with the delighted screams of little ones and their onlooking mums. The plague on the statue said: *To all women who anonymously write their story.*

Steps walked: 35,923
Camino distance travelled: 22.93kms
Total elevation ascents: 487m
Total descents: 505m

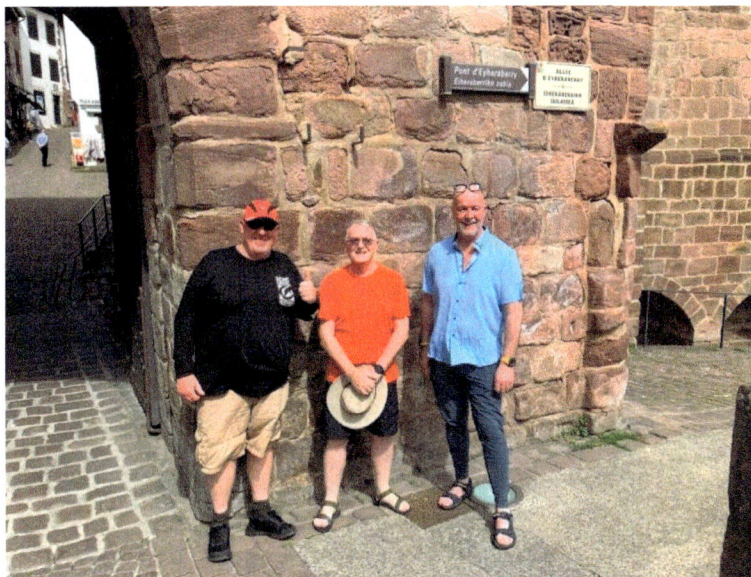

Popper, me and Paddy - Day Minus-1 - Saint-Jean-Pied-de-Port

The view of the Pyrenees, from StJPdP – They don't look too high…

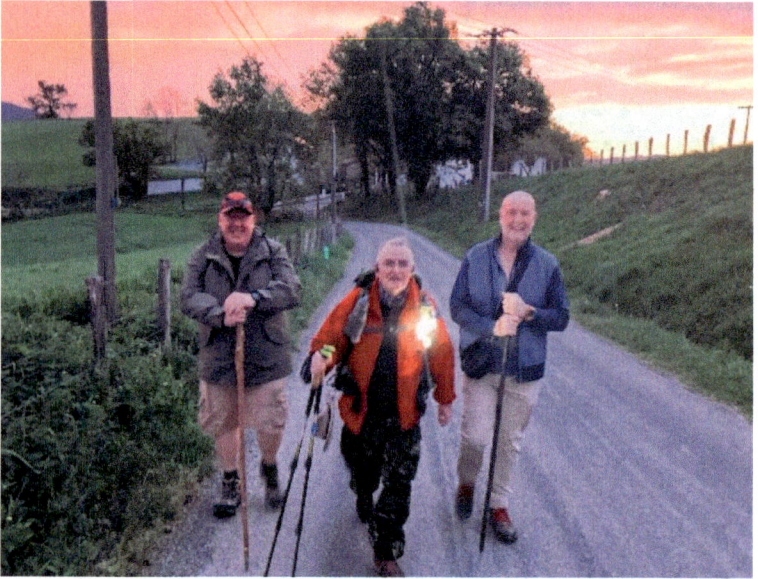

And so we start – Day 1 – StJPdP to Roncesvalles

The leading edge of the storm moving into the Pyrenees

Roncesvalles and the 'famous' sign,
with the road distance to Santiago marked

The bridge into Zubiri after a long and hard descent

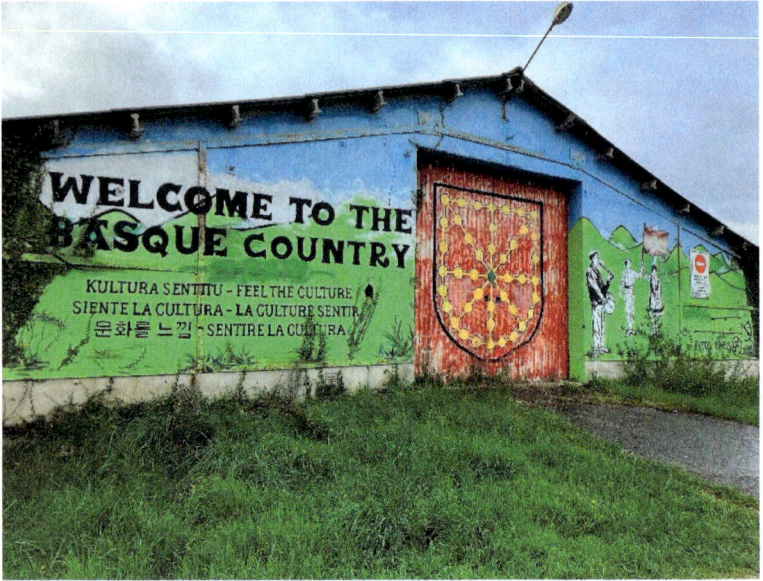

Hello (or Kaixo, pronounced Ki Shoo) in Euskara

A Pamplona morning

The Church of St. Andrew in Zariquiegui

Three modern pilgrims at the Pilgrim Sculptures

Monument of the Alto del Perdón or the Pilgrim Sculptures

The view from the top of the Queen's bridge in Puente la Reina

Sunny Spain in Spring

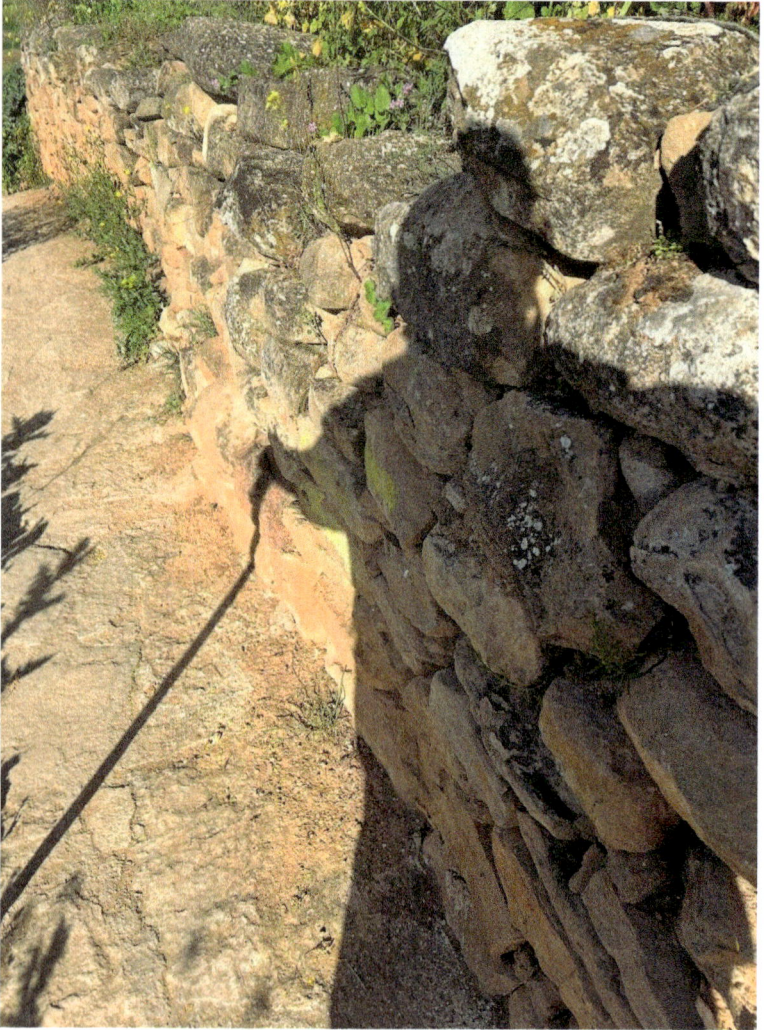

Apparently, Colin's shadow on a Roman road…
But what do you see?

Serena sketching in the Estella main square

Serena's drawing from under the bridge in Puente la Reina,
by kind permission of Serena Smart, @art.by.smart (Instagram)

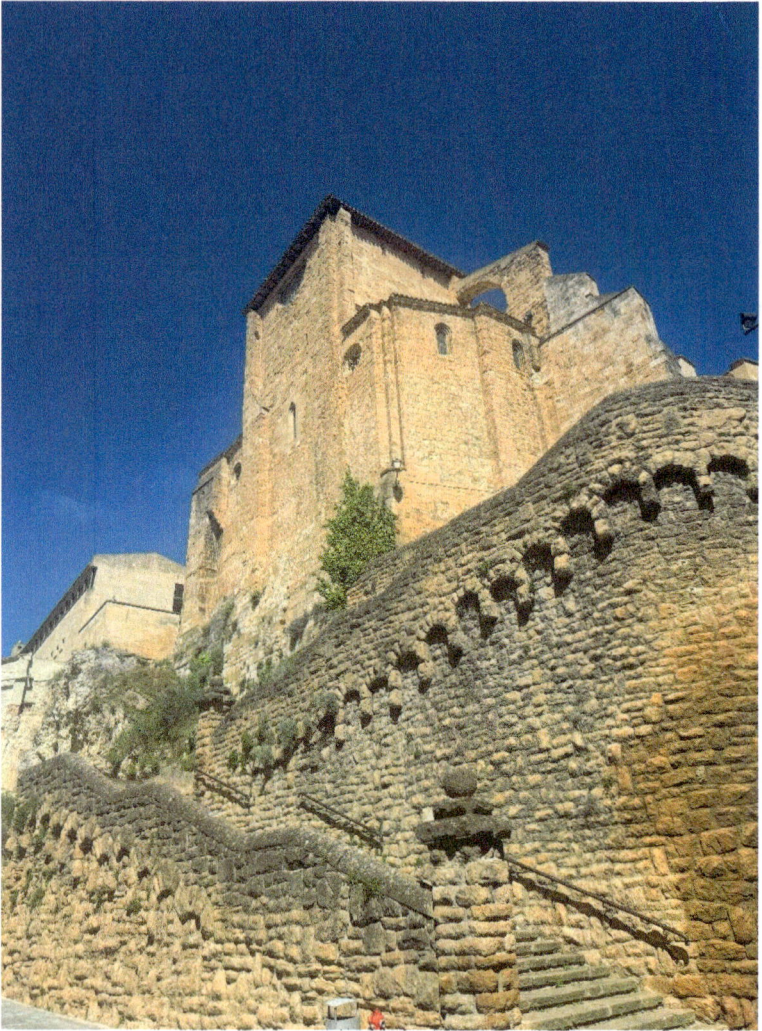

The dominating Iglesia de San Miguel on the road out of Estella

Paddy sampling the Fuente del Vino

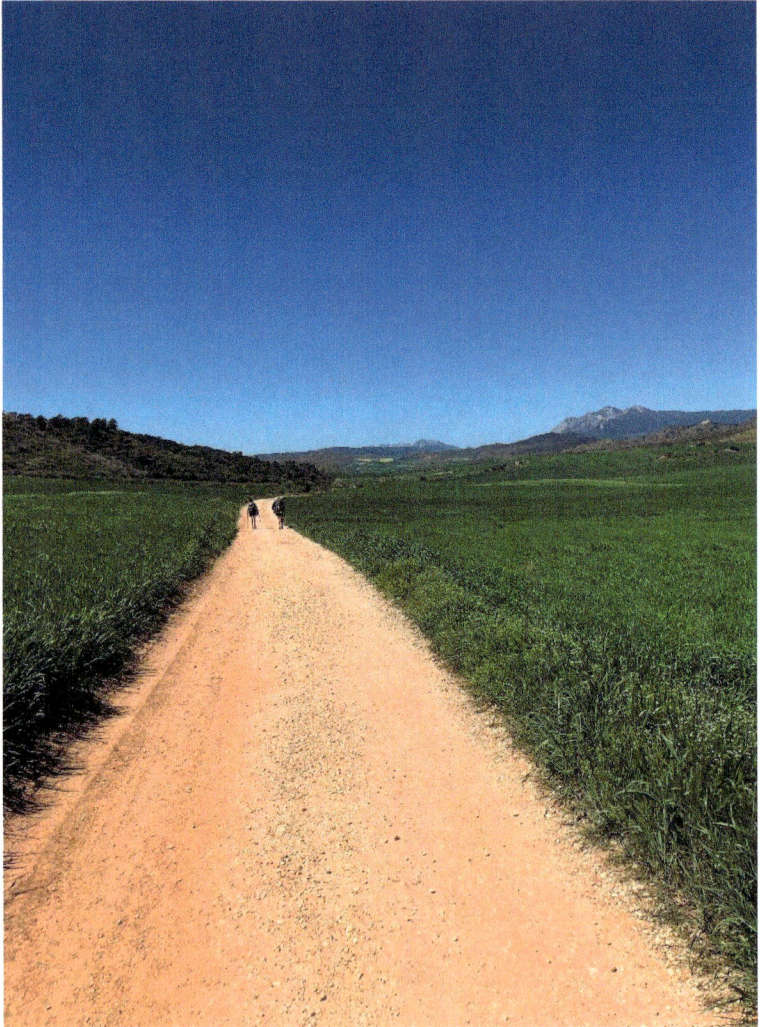

The long and not so winding road

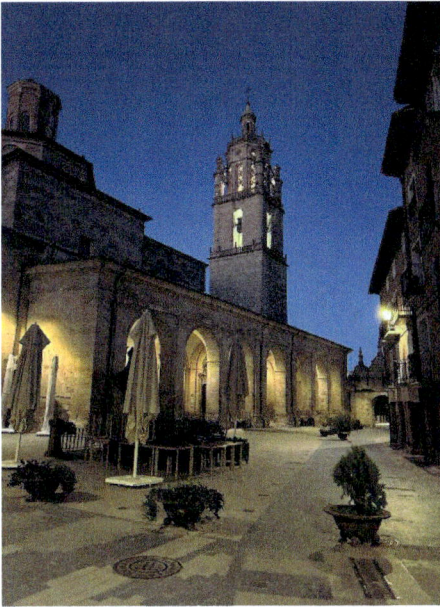

Iglesia de Santa María de Los Arcos, or the Church of Saint Mary of the Arches in Los Arcos

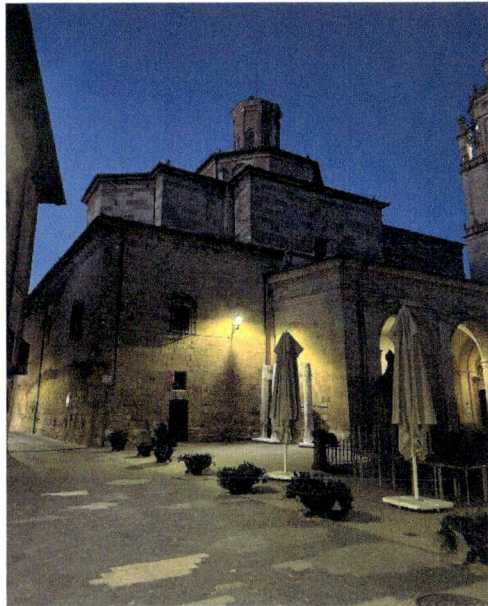

Iglesia de Santa María de Los Arcos, or the Church of Saint Mary of the Arches in Los Arcos

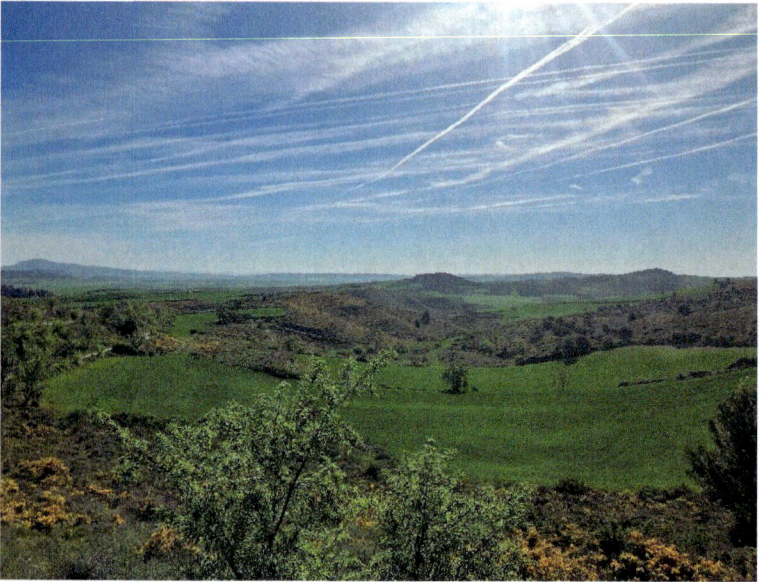

The 'PLANES' of Spain – Contrails in the Sky

Cathedral Markets in Logroño

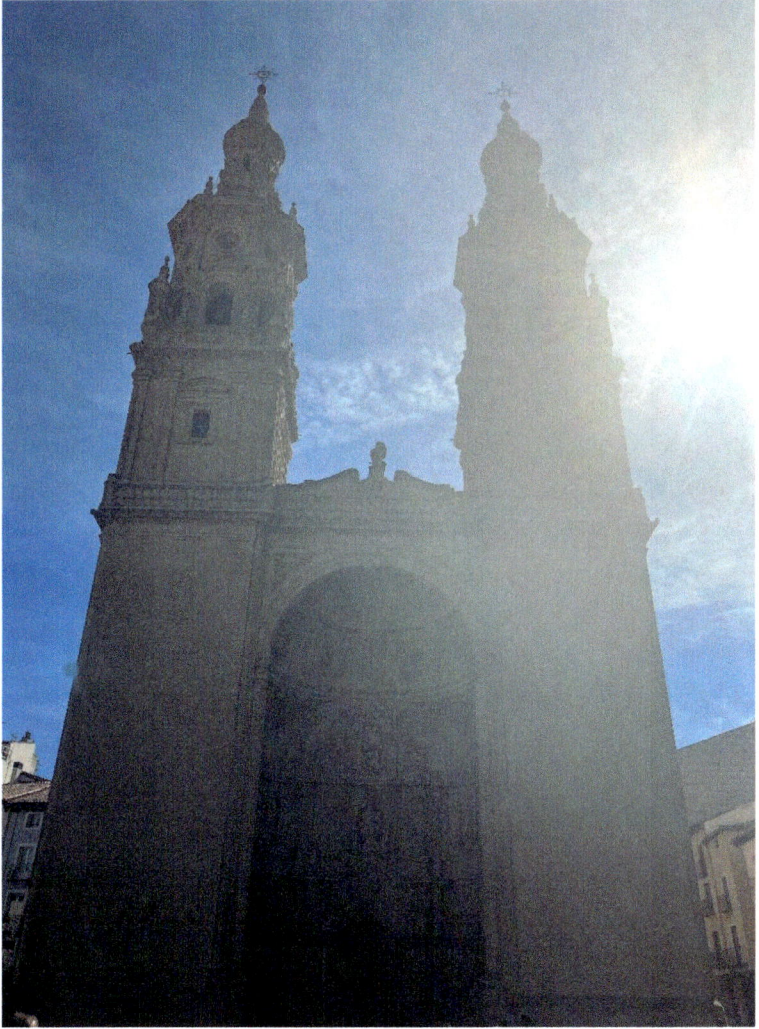

Concatedral de Santa María de la Redonda in Logroño

Harry Potter mural in Belorado

Shoemaker mural in Belorado

Us three in Burgos

The view from my apartment balcony in Burgos

Napoleon's former 'digs' in Astorga

Craigyhill in the House of Tepa, Astorga

A new stick, a new start. Paddy and his staff in Astorga

On the road again

Destination – Foncebadón – Head for the hills

A Foncebadón morning, above the clouds

Patrick (Paddy)

Colin (Popper)

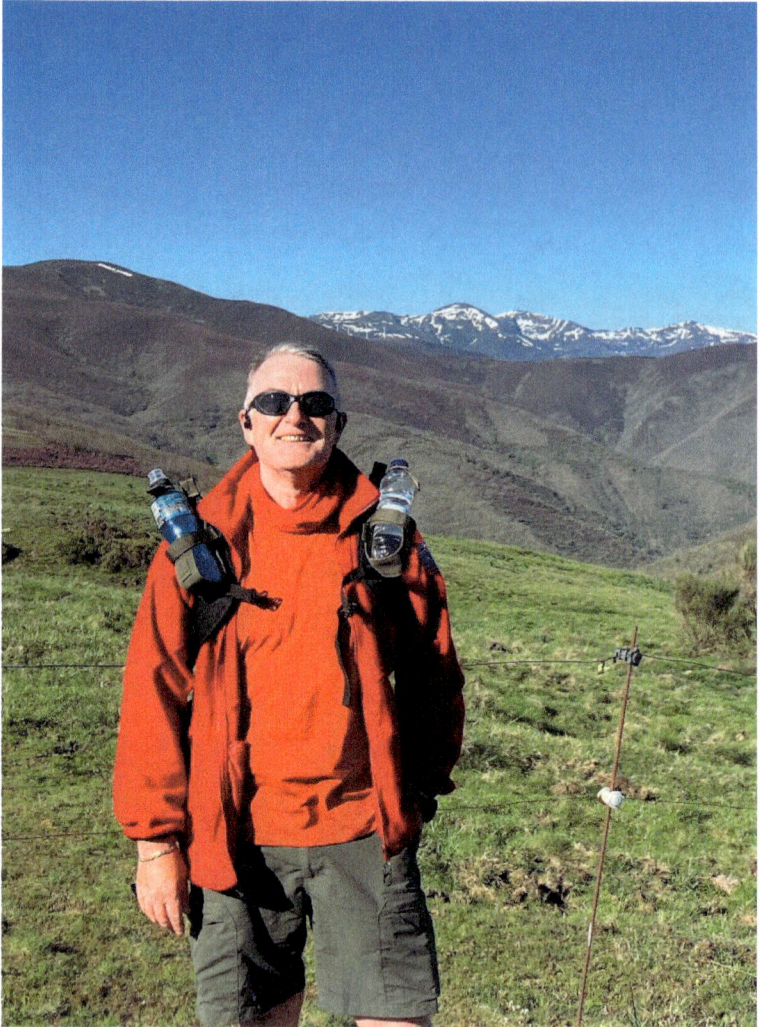

Ian (Hoops) or just… me!

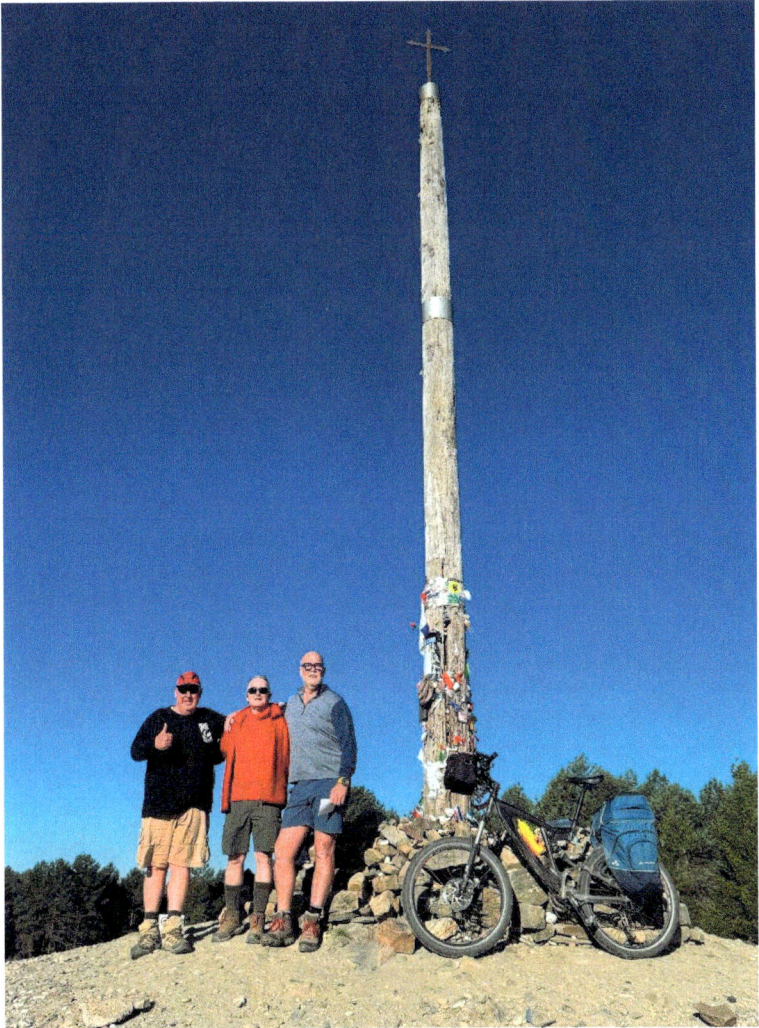

Cruz de Ferro (and a stranger's bike)

Treacherous descents

The Templar Castle

ANZAC Day Dawn – A fitting display

Crossing into Galicia – Celtic Spain

The chestnut tree of Ramil, (Castanho de Ramil) near Triacastela

The moo cows of Ramil

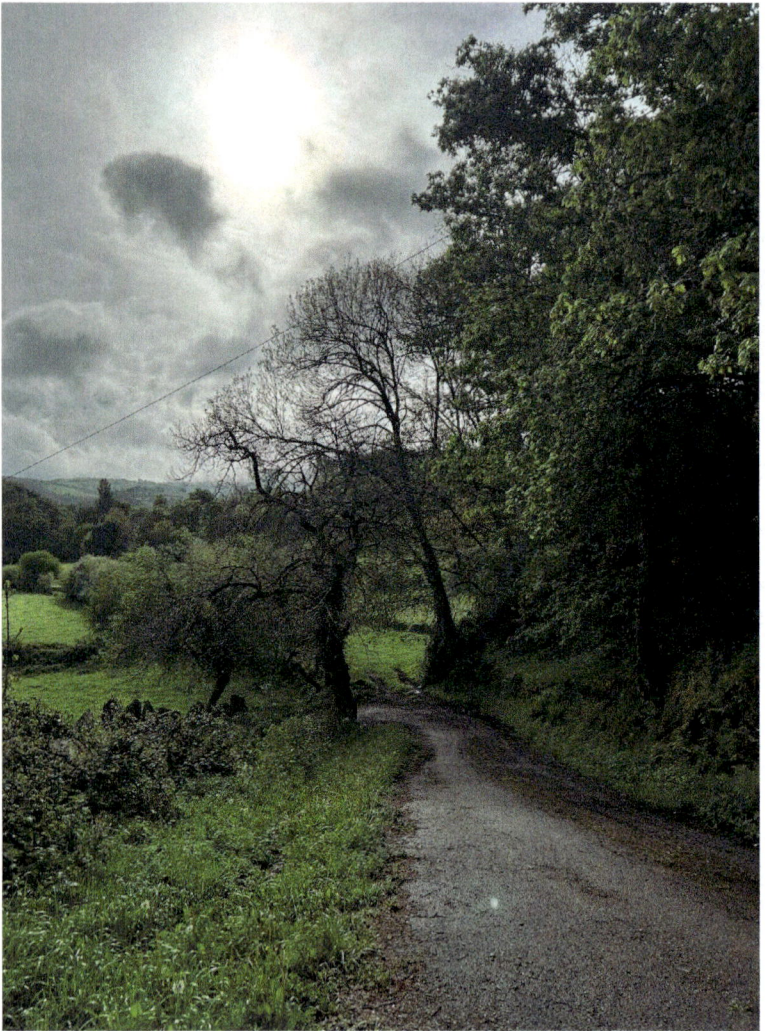

I know, a non-descript picture of a bland piece of countryside, but this was my birthday and the smell of the rainy ground and the songs of the birds just here, were enthralling. Take my word for it!

No explanation needed!

Mark (Just Mark, no nickname!)

A wet old day entering into Portomarín

Pasta in Palais de Rei

Happiness is not having a blister on your little toe (yet)

The scenic bridge into Melide

A majestic tree appears from the morning mists near O Pedrouzo

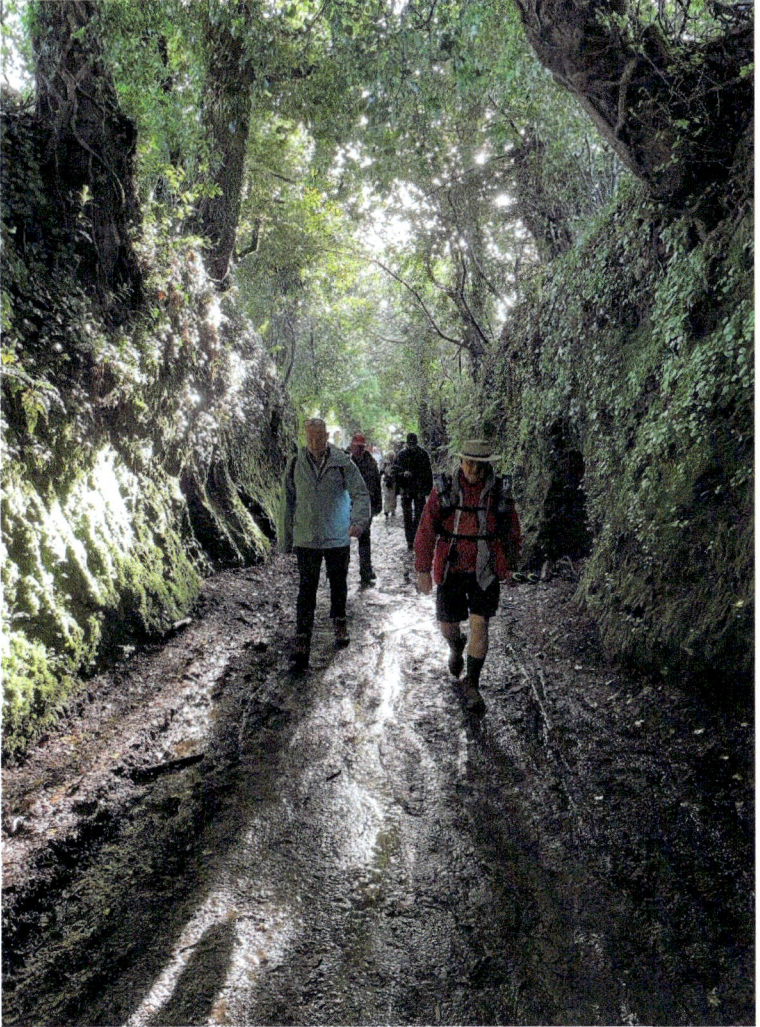

Last stretches through ancient gulleys

An iconic marker 10km out of Santiago and one which we had to queue up at to take photos

On the outskirts of Santiago

The steps down into the cathedral square

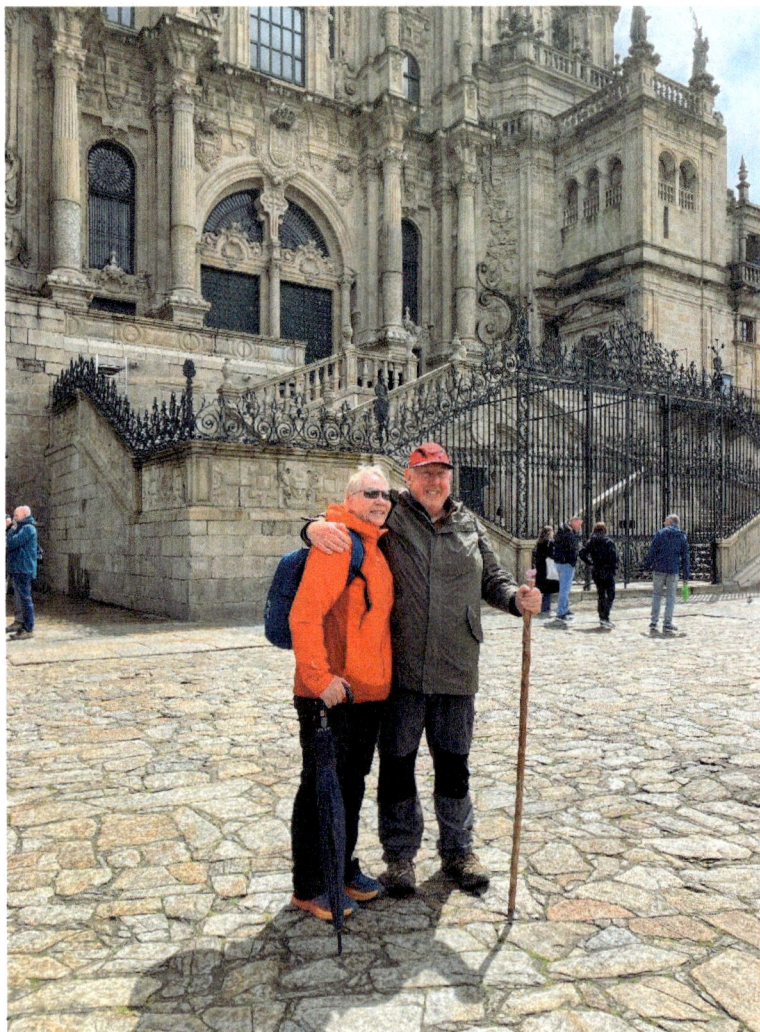

Michelle and Popper reunited – both now Camino 'veterans'

Me, Popper, Paddy, Mark and Belen – Camino Completed!

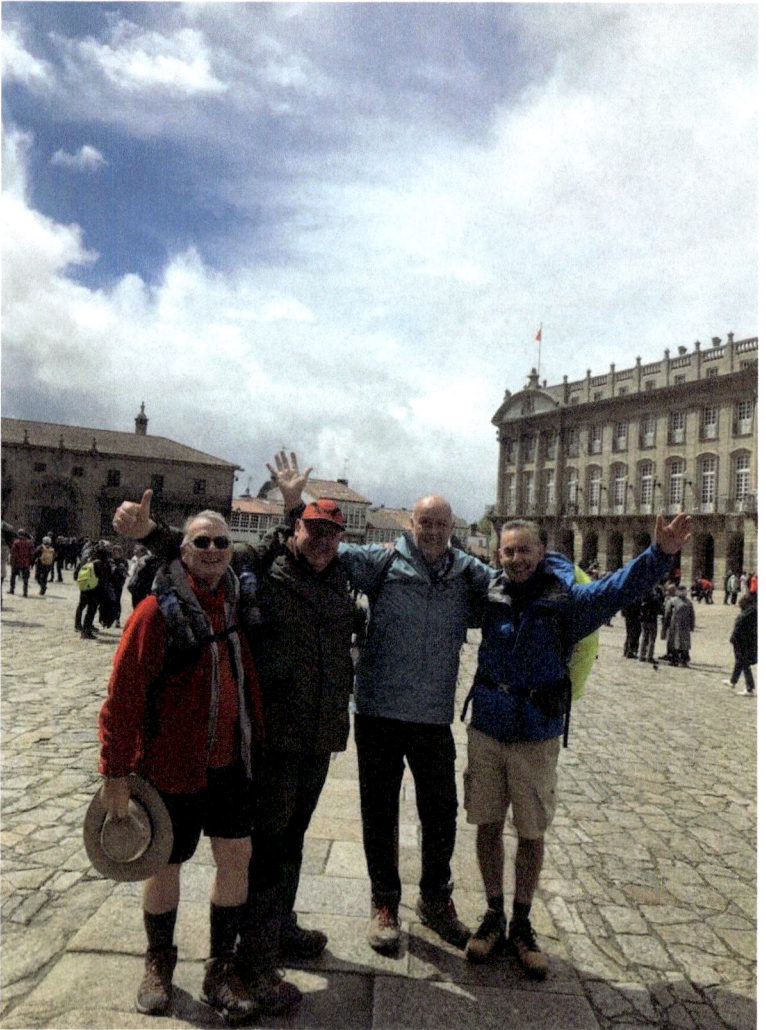

From Craigyhill to Compostela – The craic was mighty!

Day 8

April 13th 2024
Los Arcos - Logroño
Planned distance: 28km

Sometimes, as Camille could no doubt testify to, things don't go as expected. I woke in the morning with a blister on the outside of my left heel. It made no sense. My boots hadn't rubbed the day before, nor on any other days. It took me a few minutes to realise it had been my sandal. The lightweight Teva sandals that I had worn for months had never caused me an issue, but then again, I had never worn them for almost 3,000 steps following a day of wearing boots for almost 23kms. I supposed my foot had been 'softer' after being in the boot all day and then having a shower. The saving grace was that it was halfway up the outside of my heel rather on the pad of my foot or on the underside of the heel itself.

Back in the dim distant past, the best you could hope for was a band aid. Nowadays, there are incredible blister treatments available. The ones I had, and thoroughly recommended by all sources, were Compeed®. It goes on like a silicon second skin and you leave it on until it drops off in its own good time.

I stuck one on, made a coffee in the room and wolfed down a croissant or two. Packed up my kit so Jaco Trans could come grab it and set off into the pre-dawn to meet up with Paddy and Popper.

The morning stillness in Los Arcos was almost spiritual and the atmosphere was added to as I passed by the *Iglesia de Santa María de Los Arcos*, the Church of Saint Mary of the Arches. Listed as one of the most important in Navarre I am a little annoyed with myself that

I didn't go inside it the night before. Apparently the interior is worth seeing, yet my experience of the exterior in the early morning was no less rich. The Plateresque façade, the bell tower and the gallery of seven semicircular arches were all illuminated by subtle, atmospheric lighting that cast a ghostly, yet calming air all around the Plaza de Santa María. I later learned that had we been a few weeks later, on April 23, then, as it does on two occasions during the year, the sun illuminates the face of the statue of the Virgin at dusk.

Padding quietly through the streets, the bells of Los Arcos tolled for 7:00am and the birds, sensing sunrise, began to awaken with their chorus. Paddy and Popper and I met up again and continued on what we expected to be a long day of almost 28kms. In actuality, it was even longer as occasionally the guidebooks are just a little out.

Yet the morning sunrise over poppy-laden verges and lightening skies that brightened to an eggshell blue were worth every step. And the sky itself was enthralling; criss-crossed by the most aircraft contrails I've ever seen. There were literally hundreds of them diffusing across the blue, and stretching out to broad and expansive horizons. Obviously this part of Spain must be a preferred corridor for trans-Atlantic and trans-African flights. It was reminiscent of (if much less confused and far less violent than) the famous WWII photograph taken during the Battle of Britain by War Office official photographer, Captain Len A. Puttnam. These trails were to be a feature of the next few days on the Camino.

The walk today was a definite mixed bag. Long, hot with beautiful scenery and amazing skies at the start, but then a bit of a disaster at about 6.5kms. We pulled up at the tiny *Tienda Colmado*, in Sansol, a small shop whose proprietor mustn't trust anyone as he keeps the counter firmly closed and if you want something, you ask for (or point at) it. Popper said he had a small problem with his foot. When he took off his boot, it was more than a small problem. Perhaps they were catching, for he had a massive blister on the pad of his foot. I reached into my daypack for my first-aid kit, only to discover that after sorting out my own foot this morning, I must have put it into my main backpack, which was now on its way to Logroño. As we were contemplating what to do, Rat-Tail, from back in Zubiri, turned up. He had been in my periphery for the last few days, but I had avoided walking with, or talking to, him. Now here he was, offering 'help' to us. Within three sentences he managed to insult Popper, criticise Paddy and anger me to the point where I came close to breaking all the calm *bonhomie* of the Camino and punching him in the throat. I was saved from being stupid by the arrival of Ignazio, who stepped in and offered us his first-aid supplies.

There's a lot of discussion about the management of blisters. It basically comes down to two schools of thought. To Pop or Not To Pop. I am a Not To, because that's how I was trained and to pop risks infection. But Spain is not a crummy infected jungle, so you can probably safely pop without fear your foot will fall off. Popper, aptly for his nickname was, a pop them type. Therefore, I put a needle pulling thread through the blister, drained as much as I could and applied a dressing. Yet the truth was that another 22km today would potentially be the end of Popper's Camino. Fortuitously, tomorrow was one of our scheduled rest days. If he leapfrogged forward to Logroño, he could have almost 48-hours to rest and be better (or at least better than now) to resume on Monday. And Michelle, his wife, was also there so she could look after him. The decision was made, he'd get a taxi and Paddy and I would press on.

With about 12km to go, Paddy and I stopped for lunch in the narrow streets of Viana. A strange site is the *Calle Rúa Santa María* and indeed other streets in other towns on the Camino. There's not many places in the world where the sight of people resting, having a drink and something to eat, whilst taking their boots and socks off and inspecting their feet for damage goes unnoticed or uncommented on, yet here it is normal. Passing locals, going to and from church services, kids playing ball and pilgrims with their feet airing.

Sitting outside the Café Rua, we joined the two Luxembourgers and shared a few beers. Next to us, but not in the conversation, were a couple of German women, both tall and athletic. Finishing their lunch, they swung their substantial backpacks up like they were no weight at all and set off at a brisk pace. A chorus of Buen Caminos rang out to help them on their way. About five minutes later, I realised one of them had forgotten their trekking poles. The proprietor also saw the poles and took them in for 'safe keeping'. I convinced him the women were unlikely to return but we might bump into them on the road. I couldn't quite see how we were going to catch them, but perhaps our paths would cross. In the interim, *sans-staff* Paddy would have a stick to replace his missing one. Two sticks in fact.

We may have sat longer and had a few more beers than first planned. Eventually, Paddy decided he would get a bus or a taxi through to Logroño, to see how Popper was doing.

I decided to walk on and meet them later. The morning's scenery, wide skies and distant horizons had been great. I figured more of that would be good for me, and it would have been, except the afternoon road was not the same. The final 11.7kms were akin to walking through an oven and as with most big cities, Logroño's outskirts were distinctly 'industrial' in function and views. The only bright point was walking the last kilometre or so in the company of Ignazio.

Thankfully, it ended at the Hotel Gran Via. One of our stopover rest day hotels and therefore a bit of a step up in price (and luxury). On the last kilometre of the day, I had started wishing for a bath to soak my legs and feet in. Every other accommodation to date had only showers, terrific as they'd been, so I wasn't hopeful. Ah, but the Camino provides and sure enough, the room came with a long low bath. I was very happy.

Once sorted, we four, now Michelle was here, all met up. The strangest revelation was that it had taken hours to walk from Sansol, but Popper had made the taxi journey in about 20 minutes. The distances that seemed great, weren't.

Michelle, Popper and Paddy wanted to attend evening mass in *La concatedral de Santa María de la Redonda* (The Co-Cathedral of Saint Mary of the Round – the round being a reference to the shape of an earlier church on the site.), so I set off to find something to eat and a phone repair shop, to have a new screen protector fitted.

I am a little embarrassed to say that prior to the Camino, I had never heard of Logroño. Yet it's a big city, thriving and thronged. The phone shop was found in less than ten minutes, as was a place called Crepecatessen, that unsurprisingly, specialised in crepes, but oh! What an array of them. All sorts of savoury and sweet fillings. I could hardly move after a cheddar cheese, shredded chicken, bacon, fried onions and barbecue sauce crepe followed by a small, sweet crepe with vanilla ice cream.

Finished, I waddled around the corner, contemplated the Irish Bar fronting onto the main plaza, decided against it and elected instead to go with the alfresco seating of a bar opposite the cathedral's side entrance. A Grolsch Radler and a front row seat on the passing populace. It was simultaneously great to feel the atmosphere engendered by thousands of people and a little overwhelming after the almost total isolation of the Way. Logroño seemed to be quite a party city. However, after today's kilometres and the crepes, that was the last thing I needed. Before my Grolsch arrived, I nipped over the road to take in the quite magnificent interior of the cathedral.

I gave a wave to P[2] and Michelle, motioned I'd meet them outside when they were done and then returned to my beer. My phone pinged to reveal that our hometown team, Larne Football Club, had won 8-1 against the third placed team in the league. Perfect.

Steps walked: 45,838 (New PB, included wandering around the city)
Camino distance travelled: 30.19kms
Total elevation ascents: 670m
Total descents: 724m

Day 9

April 14th 2024
Logroño – Rest Day
Planned distance: None

On this glorious Sunday in Spain, I wondered if, when not writing about walking the Camino, I was meant to write lyrically.

Perhaps I should be trying to mimic one of my favourite authors, Laurie Lee, in the description of the vistas of Spain. Give insight to the narrow side streets of the city, once blank in their austerity, now vibrant with a kaleidoscopic mix of spray-can colours portraying no artistic merit individually, yet in the clash and mix of 'tags' somehow replicating Spain's famous Cubist son.

How theses streets buzzed with the noise of humanity so unlike the open roads and pathways of the countryside. That harmonious midtone buzz, underpinned by the bass of traffic hum, highlighted by top notes of melodic church bells calling the faithful to their Mass.

Or how in the late morning, sitting in the square outside the main cathedral, those angelic bells washed over a rag tag, higgledy-piggledy collection of market stalls that sold antiques of dubious authenticity, bric-a-brac, books and clocks, toys and zodiacs. I could tell you how, from my seat out front of the Mercado Café, I was reminded of passages from the New Testament, you know… the ones about the money changers and the temple.

The truth is a lot less lyrical. As I had my first coffee in a week, rather than launching into a seriously pale imitation of 'Lee-esque' proportions, dwelling on the cyclical nature of life and spirituality, I instead tried to work out why temperatures are weird.

This might seem trivial, but I am perplexed. I now live in Western Australia and have often been aware that 15 to 18°C there feels so much colder than that temperature ever did in Northern Ireland. I put it down to being acclimatised to WA heat, but these past few days in Spain have averaged 25 to 27°C. That is a pleasant, almost perfect day in WA. Here though, it has felt like walking through an oven. The sun seems 'stronger' and the heat is more intense, even when not walking. I don't understand it. Is it ozone layers or the tilt of the planet? Is it all in my head? That and other deep and meaningful thoughts accompanied me on my meanders around Logroño today. The city is beautiful. I walked further than I should on a rest day, but it was worth it. Especially for one reason in particular.

It is an odd, yet beautiful and comforting thing to wander through a strange city and be occasionally greeted by familiar faces. Fellow pilgrims who call your name. Welcoming smiles and warm, "Hellos," a quick swapping of mutual updates on feet, legs, next stops and then to walk on. I found myself smiling a lot.

The first encounter was with Clara (Alaskan Bear Clara) and her niece. This was their last day. They'd be going back home tomorrow. We parted like we'd know each other for years. Then Camille, much better now and looking forward to the rest of her Camino stage. Keith and John, who smiled when I told them our bags were being transported on a daily basis.

(By the way, Popper and Paddy are convinced Keith and John do not work in their stated professions of newspapers and refuse disposal, but are undercover Special Branch cops trailing us on our Camino). I think with half a chance, Paddy and Popper could write better crime novels than me.

Sadly, I didn't run into Ignazio. He'd messaged me to say that he'd been unable to find accommodation in Logroño the previous evening and had gone on through to Navarette. A total one-day distance from Los Arcos of 42km. That's a marathon. What with our rest day, and him moving on, our Caminos wouldn't cross paths again, but I think that is one of the joys of this. A changing cast on an ever-changing stage and backdrop.[3]

My companions and I met up for dinner. Huge shout out to *La Tagliatella* (with an 'a' not an 'e') an Italian restaurant in Logroño. If you get a chance, go. Can't recommend it highly enough. A great end to an enjoyable day.

Steps walked: 17,114 (Probably more than I should have)
Camino distance travelled: Not applicable
Total elevation ascents: Not counting the hotel lifts - minimal
Total descents: As above

---

[3] Ignazio would finish his Camino on 12 May having raised over £5000 for MND.

Day 10

April 15th 2024
Logroño – Nájera
Planned distance: 29kms

Alas every day cannot be overwhelmingly picturesque and this one wasn't, yet later in the afternoon we were confronted by a faraway dramatic beauty.

At 07:00, with the sun still thinking about making an appearance, we bade farewell to Michelle and left Logroño town centre, out through the parks and gardens surrounding it, onwards to Navarette, Ventosa and thence on to Nájera.

Across from the town church in Navarette, our first stop of the day was the small *Bocateria* bar, café and albergue, another great little place on the Way. Tiny on the inside, this was where I had been siting, enjoying tea and toast when Paddy came in and said, "You should go and look at the church next door, it's amazing."

"I will, I'll just finish this."

As I drank the last of my tea, I was joined by Joy and her companion, (who I know was a relative of hers, but I can't recall if it was her granddaughter or niece, apologies if they are reading this). We talked about our backgrounds and they asked me how I'd got into writing. I told them I'd started off by writing silly poems and daft rhymes. Turns out it was Joy's 70th birthday. I wished her many happy returns and said it was a shame I hadn't known as I'd have at least tried to write an 'Ode to Joy'. Everyone laughed, I grabbed my kit and went off to see the chapel Paddy had enthused about. He was right to have enthused.

La iglesia de Santa María de la Asunción the Church of Saint Mary of the Assumption in Navarette, is stunning and more so as it was unexpected for a tiny town to have such a 'wealth' of an interior in their place of worship. The altarpiece is overwhelming, listed as one of the largest in the world, it occupies the space from floor to ceiling of the apse and is covered with gilded reliefs and polychrome figures. The sheer amount of gilding is something to behold.

As in most churches, there was a silent, referential atmosphere, yet I could, once my ears became attuned to the acoustics, detect the gentlest rhythms of background music being played through the chapel's interior speakers. So low was the volume that it needed concentration to pick it up. I almost laughed out loud, turned on my heel and stepped the ten paces back to the café.

Sitting down beside Joy again, I said, "You won't believe me, but if you are quick and go into the church, you might be surprised."

"Oh, why's that?"

"They have music playing in there. It's Beethoven's Symphony No. 9."

Her travelling companion laughed. "You're kidding?"

"Nope, Beethoven's *Ode to Joy*. Playing at a church near you."

As I rose to leave, I had to stand to one side as a women came in with about four backpacks on each arm. There was a van outside with Jaco Trans written on the side of it.

She stopped and smiled. Small and obviously strong, her head was completely shaved and she looked so happy, that it was impossible not to smile back at her as she adjusted the bags and prepared to go up the staircase of the little café.

"You must be Jaco?" I joked.

"Oh, no, I'm Barbara. Nice to meet you," she replied in faultless English before heading up to drop the packs into the albergue part of Bocateria. Paddy, Popper and I, with our lighter daypacks shouldered for the road, figured our own heavier backpacks were probably in the back of Barbara's van and we set off happy.

Despite the countryside being a bit 'samey' for the majority of the day, as the afternoon drew on, we were confronted by the grandeur of a wide bowl landscape surrounded by distant mountains that seemed busy making towering cloud formations which swelled and rose to dominate the distant horizons. Huge white breakers standing off against deep, dark blankets, both threatening rain which, thankfully, avoided us completely. Above me was only blue skies and drifts of thin white trails. Like I was in the middle of a cloudy tonsure.

I found myself focusing on the small things you notice when walking. Flowers (I had no idea what type, but was later told on Social Media they had been blue cornflowers), a farmer who obviously 'loved' his tractor and had a personal number plate of LO-VE, - alas it wasn't really a personalised number plate, just the standard plate for the region around here, but it made me laugh for a while on a flat and otherwise lacklustre stretch of the road, and an inspiring graffiti wit who had written above the word Stop on a traffic sign: Don't, and below it: Walking.

Given the three of us were walking in isolation for most of today (down to our different pace lengths and speeds) I reverted for the first time to my Spotify playlist. It's as eclectic a list of music genres and artists as I thought might keep me entertained on the walk and I was delighted with my bone conduction headphones. They give a reasonable fidelity, but crucially permit a large degree of situational awareness, important when walking on open roads. Today I discovered that the pipes of the Scot's Guards playing *Marie's Wedding* are good to help me walk down rolling hills beside fields of vineyards and that *Black Magic* by Little Mix is good at getting me back up the other side. The music made the day shorter but almost 30km was still a test.

As I arrived into Nájera, walking down towards my apartment

and knowing that Paddy and Popper were going to be in a small hotel on the other side of the river, I saw 'Jaco Trans' Barbara approaching.

"Hello Barbara."

She stopped and gave me a quizzical look. "Um, hello."

"Sorry, I saw you in Navarette this morning, dropping off bags."

"Oh, yes, I remember. Are you staying in Nájera?"

"Yep, in a small apartment called Vino Y Camino. Hopefully you dropped my bag there and my mates' bags in the Hotel Hispano."

She frowned. "I know the Vino Y Camino, but I haven't dropped a bag there today. Nor Hispano. Where were the bags coming from?"

"The Gran Via, Logroño?"

She frowned again. The resultant conversation revealed that no, Barbara hadn't picked the bags up. She hadn't been told about the bags. The hotel hadn't contacted her for a pick-up and, as it said on every Jaco Trans envelope, it was up to the client to contact them.

A few things fell out of this bizarre and random encounter on the street. Without it, I would never have known what happened to our bags and we would have been … insert whatever word you want here, the only ones I could think of both then and now are rude.

My mobile, whilst having data on it, did not have Spanish call time on it and the hotel wasn't on WhatsApp. My Spanish was passable, but nowhere near fluent enough to deal with this.

Barabara pulled out her mobile phone and made the call. I duly authorised the hotel to order a taxi to bring all our bags to my apartment, the address of which turned out to be four doors up from where Barbara and her family lived.

I thanked her profusely, she told me, kindly but firmly, that I must contact the Jaco Trans every day to tell them about pick-ups and drop-offs, I agreed. I thanked her again; she said it was her pleasure to have been able to help and how lucky it was that she had been going to collect her daughter from school at the same time as I had been walking into the town. I agreed again.

As we parted, I reflected on the 'luck' needed for Paddy to have recommended for me to go and see the interior of a church. How I had heard some music playing and because of it, had returned to a café to share a joke about Ode to Joy with a lady called Joy, who happened to be celebrating her 70th birthday. Had it not been for that series of events, I wouldn't have seen Barbara initially and wouldn't have recognised her on this street. I pondered on the ability of the Camino to provide.

About thirty minutes later the taxi from Logroño turned up. It was both pleasing to have been so quick and soul destroying to know how long the day's walk had taken us. Or perhaps that should be sole-destroying.

With bags secured, I checked-in to the Vino Y Camino apartment. What can I tell you that isn't going to sound repetitively boring? The décor was… Yellow. Very yellow. But the kitchen was great, the place was clean, and yes, the shower was fantastic.

It had been a long day and the slight hiccup with the bags made for a tiring end to it. Nájera is a small place with some good eateries, an amazing landscape and one of the most impressive monasteries you'll see on the Camino: the *Santa María la Real Monastery*. Other than the *La Mercería Restaurante*, which was cheap, fast and filling, I saw none of it. I retired to the apartment and went to bed.

Tomorrow would be a new day.

Steps walked: 44,333
Camino distance travelled: 29.71kms
Total elevation ascents: 571m
Total descents: 484m

Day 11

April 16th 2024
Nájera - Santo Domingo de la Calzada
Planned distance: 21kms

Ach! Today was wheeker so it was. Which is Northern Irish for, "Ah, today was great!"

Calling on my vast knowledge of geography, I can safely say, Spain is lumpy. Some of it is very lumpy indeed, some less so. Today was a less so day. The scenery not that dissimilar from yesterday, with ranges of mountains looking down from distant horizons and broad fields of green and yellows stretching away to them. Yet today was about names and coincidences, and being, once more, in the right place at the right time.

Let's begin as I left the town of Nájera. Like I said, I'd been tired last night and to be fair to myself, I hadn't realised about the town's monastery until I was walking past it in the morning. Having discovered the magnificent building, I was a little annoyed at myself for not seeking it out, but you can only do so much and sometimes sleep wins.

Anyway, here I was now and could at least take in the exterior and read all the tourist notices posted about it. According to legend, it was founded in 1052 by king Don García Sánchez III, after he saw a mysterious image of the Virgin Mary in a nearby cave.

Today's surviving church dates from 1516 and apparently has three naves and a transept. From the church you can still gain access to the cave where the king found the image of the Virgin. A Baroque altarpiece in the main chapel dates from the end of the 17th century and the choir stalls are from the beginning of the 16th. There was a lot more detail about the inside and I do wish I'd seen the ancient tombs of the kings of the Kingdom of Nájera-Pamplona, the precursor to the Kingdom of Navarra. Ah well, maybe next time. I made do with a few photos of the exterior and pressed on.

Not far from the town's outskirts I was bracketed by Dr Rhonda (Venezuela, but moved to Texas as a newly qualified doctor almost 50 years ago) and her buddy, insurance agent, Josie (Mexico, now Texas). I know the town they're from in Texas thanks to a Marty Robbins' song. I complimented them on their hats. They tried to gift them to me. I spent a good few minutes telling them they were far to kind, but no, I was fine for hats and to be honest, they suited them much better than me. Only when they were sure I was sure, did they relent.

We spent about ten minutes chatting, and they kindly schooled me in 'Latin American' Spanish. They were very patient and taught me how to order 'black tea' properly, a thing I had been struggling with for days. I didn't want green tea and had tried, brown tea with milk and sugar, breakfast tea with the same and tea tea, none of which had got more than confused looks and so I'd reverted either to English or pointing. Now, thanks to their patience I knew how to say, "*té negro con leche y azúcar.*" Rhonda and Josie are also doing their Camino in sections. Another stretch each year. This is their third. I bade them, "Adios," and meandered on alone as Paddy, Popper and I were as usual strung out along the Way. Six kilometres in, I had my first break of the morning. A few pilgrims bunched up as usual, including Paddy Popper and me.

Sitting down with a cup of tea at *Bar Restaurante El Descanso del Peregrino,* the Pilgrim's Rest Bar & Restaurant in Azofra, I was joined at an outside table by a lady called Wendy who was walking the Camino to celebrate her 80th year. Noticing my Australian shoulder patch, she asked in a polite, refined accent, "Ah, Australia, where from exactly?"

Australia's a big place and most people only know Sydney and Melbourne, so when being asked, I tend to be less than specific.

'Western Australia, south of Perth.'

"Oh, where?"

"You know WA?"

"Yes I live …" she mentioned a town 25km from mine.

"Wow! I live in Leschenault. Near Bunbury."

"That's my surname," she said.

"Sorry?"

"Bunbury. That's my surname."

And that is how Wendy Bunbury and I sat and enjoyed a cup of properly ordered black tea in the Spanish town of Azofra, about 14,500kms from the town she is a namesake of. Wendy was also raising funds for the Perron Institute's research goals, coincidentally also involving MND research.

I finished my tea and once more meandered on. About 10km later, at the foot of a long rise, I stopped for a drink of water and a snack to prep for the rising ground. Two French ladies sat on the grassy verge smoking. Ah, I recall that as an equally effective way to prepare for waking up a big hill. The nearest one saw the flag and asked, "Australia? Where from?"

"Western Australia, just south of Perth."

She opened the map app on her phone and looked for Perth as she continued in flawless English, "I have been to Sydney. Wow, it is a long way from Perth," she said. "Where are you?" She offered her phone and I zoomed in to the region where I live.

"Non!!" She yelped.

"What?"

"That is my surname."

"What??"

"Lechenault. That is my surname."

And so it was. Albeit without the S in Leschenault.

I mean, if I was making it up you wouldn't believe it.

She had one of the pieces of kit that I'd looked at but hadn't bought: the Ultralight folding foam 'Sit Pad'. As the title says, it's an ultra-lightweight foam 'seat' to keep you dry when resting along the trail. I asked if it was any good. She confirmed it was and then tried, like Rhonda and Josie had with their hats, to gift it to me. Once more it took a bit of persuading to convince her that I was just enquiring.

I bade them farewell, climbed the hill and eventually, 5km later, paused at the last rest stop of the day. Sometimes the cafes and bars are quaint and rustic and sometimes you stumble upon a different class of venue. Arriving into the café of the Rioja Alta Golf Club on the outskirts of Cirueñaa was very pleasant. As I walked in, Dr Rhonda and Josie were trying to pay for two green teas. The point-of-sale machine kept rejecting their card. Wifi problems. Neither had cash on them. I figured €3.60 was a very reasonable price for my morning Spanish lesson. And so the world turned.

Parts of today looked like, 'follow the yellow brick road' or more correctly, follow the yellow dusty road, yet over the last kilometres into Santo Domingo de la Calzada it became a wide path laid with a mosaic of hexagonal pavers that looked yellow on the landscape as it wound into the distance. Up close it was more a subtle pink colour, but was probably the best maintained part of the Way we would encounter. I walked into the town in the company of Camille, whose feet were much better and she chatted about her family and her intention to do the whole Camino over the next few years.

On reaching my digs, Hostel Atuvera on Calle Mayor, top tip, read the numbers on the doors properly or you end up at the wrong end of a long street, I did my usual, prepped me and my kit for tomorrow. Except, as I took my trusty Columbia boots off, I saw they both had developed holes in the same place. On the outside edge, over where my little toe would be, between the leather toe-cap protector and the first reinforced stitching for the lace holes, there was a piece of webbing material. Now there was an extra airgap on each.

Quick Google search revealed a camping supplies shop forty metres away. Off I went, not too keen on getting new boots that would need to be broken in on the walk, but figuring I might not have much choice. If it rained, I'd be stuffed with wet feet. Perhaps I could get tape to fix them up.

I asked in fractured Spanish if the shop had any tape I could use to fix boots? The assistant, speaking better English than me, said, "You could always take them to the cobbler around the corner."

Yeah. For real. An old-fashioned shoe repairer, with a machine shop on the premises. Not a key cutting, heel repairing type of shop in a mall, but a proper cobbler, with lasts and stitches in time.

I set off. He spoke no English and my translation app decided it did indeed need a signal to work, so he and I conversed and I dragged up all the lessons Seana had taught me (or tried to). Between us we established the problem my boots had, that he was open until 8pm, that I needed to go get the boots now (I had changed into sandals and the boots were back in my digs as I hadn't fancied carrying them around town in a forlorn hope). He'd fix them, but that if I didn't come back before 8pm, he would be shut until tomorrow afternoon. Off I ran. And back I came. He took them, I found a spot nearby for dinner and as I was finishing, Tim, Deb and Camille dropped in to the restaurant. We caught up for a half hour, as if we were friends from the same small town. I guess we are. Just happens that the town's population is on the move, all going the same way. The Way.

I returned to the cobbler at 7.50pm. Boots fixed with proper over and under stitching. They'd last the trip. He asked for €15. I figured not asking for change from a twenty was a better idea and wandered back to my hotel thinking that the 'Camino Provides' wasn't a myth.

Steps walked: 36,054
Camino distance travelled: 22.81kms
Total elevation ascents: 651m
Total descents: 492m

Day 12

April 17th 2024
Santo Domingo de la Calzada – Belorado
Planned distance: 22.7km

An almost perfect walking day. Villages at regular intervals, overcast, cool temperatures, even a fine mist of fog. Scenery not fabulous, but it was as flat as a proverbial pancake and the company made the day.

I should mention that most times the company I ran into would have already walked alongside Paddy and Popper, or would walk with them later. It made for a bizarre conversation with a total stranger that would begin, after introductions, with, "Oh you're Colin's mate," or, "Ah yes, I met Paddy yesterday." So it was with Bob, who Paddy had walked alongside earlier in the day.

Bob, 73, lives in Montana. His daily scenery is the backdrop to TV series such as *Yellowstone* and *1923*. He was born in New Jersey, about 20 miles north, and a year or so after, a guy called Springsteen. Bob saw Bruce play early gigs in local bars.

Through college, Bob was an American Football player. Given his age and location, I wondered if he'd served in Vietnam, but that's not a question you ask. Veterans might tell you that they served in such and such a formation, but rarely do we offer further details about any of our tours. As it was, after a few more kilometres of chatting, he volunteered his story. On graduation there was a real potential that he would be drafted for Vietnam and rather than be given a random assignment, he decided to pre-emptively join the United States Marine Corps. With his decision made, he went to bed that night and woke to discover President Nixon had canned conscription. Bob didn't go down to the recruiting office and the war ended two years later.

A career as a coach and athletic recruiter for colleges followed, until one day he decided that the eastern states weren't where he wanted to raise his kids, so he went west and changed the direction of his life. As his story unfolded, he strode alongside me pace for pace. I realised he looked like Paul Hollywood (the bakeoff guy).

For most of the late morning we spoke of Springsteen and his albums, especially *The River* and *Nebraska*, also his one-man special on Netflix. We talked about our partners waiting at home. He told me stories of baseball and basketball, football and college drafts. He said how he'd been lucky enough to walk the first couple of days on the Camino with his youngest son.

At the last rest stop of the day, we bade farewell. His handshake in departure was strong. His bright blue eyes, full of mirth.

The last 4k of today, I walked into my destination town with the young artist from back in Estella, Serena. She's doing the Camino with a loose group, mainly from the US, who drift ahead and behind of each other but somehow always find themselves when they need to. Sure enough, when we got to Belorado she met her friends and I caught up with mine. She showed me the final versions of her sketches before departing. Seriously talented, Serena was like my amazingly artistic wife in how she modestly downplayed her skills.

Sadly, the town of Belorado was shut. Siesta time is well known in Spanish culture, but a decent entrepreneur could make a good living from us walkers if they stayed open for the usual arrival time of most pilgrims; 1-4pm in the afternoon. We want to get in, sort ourselves and our kit, and get stocked for the next day. But, when in Spain… so we wait, have dinner at 7pm, then get stocked up in the local supermarket. However, we could at least get into our accommodation. I was in Caminante, an albergue that had some rooms with private bathrooms. Yet again, clean, functional, perfect.

Paddy and Popper were across the way in a hotel that had a bar and a restaurant. The beer was cold and the food excellent. What more could you want?

Whilst at dinner we sat across from two Scottish sisters, who we'd bump into over the next few days at various rest stops. Sometimes it's nice to talk to people whose accent is so similar to one's own that you're not asked to repeat yourself!

Belorado is quite small and yet is home to another place that I am sad I didn't get a chance to see. The Museum of Radio Communication is, according to their website, '*a collection of radio communication equipment organized to mark milestones in the history, including a reproduction of the Titanic's first-class cabins as well as the radio room, the reproduction in Europe of a trench from the First World War, Checkpoint Charlie in Berlin and a helicopter and tank from the Vietnam era.*' Wow!

Yes, I am a nerd, don't judge me… It's fine. I know I am.

Missing out on it meant I did get to appreciate some more artists. The Belorado town murals are outstanding. My second favourite was on the side of a Hotel and Restaurant called *La Huella del Camino* (loosely translating as the footprints, or the trace, of the road). It showed the night sky, the Milky Way, shooting stars, a pilgrim with shell on backpack and pole in hand. Up in the top left corner was a head. A great self-portrait of the artist, I assumed, but there was no one around to ask. What was certain is that the head looked a lot like Daniel Radcliffe, of *Harry Potter* fame.

Yet the one that won for me, was the front wall of what might have been apartments, filled with a scene of a cobbler and his wife mending shoes and boots, using lasts and stitching with thread. It seemed like the perfect end to the day. And yes, my boots were fine.

Steps walked: 36,409
Camino distance travelled: 21.56kms
Total elevation ascents: 405m
Total descents: 265m

Day 13

April 18th 2024
Belorado - Atapuerca
Planned distance: 32km

We decided on a relatively early start. I say relatively as some folks are out and walking by 5 or 6am each day, but 7am would do us. It was going to be a big day of 30+kms and mountains apparently. The guide says it's one of the 'trickiest' days on the Way and we know enough now to realise the guide is an understater! Somewhere along the route today, I passed half a million steps since arriving in Paris.

Also, brrrrrr… It was cold. Very. And yet, once we got moving, it became bearable, although my fingers were blue at one point. Whose silly idea had it been to send all the cold weather kit forward to Santiago? I mean, I could have at least kept a pair of gloves.

Anyhow, the guides (books, apps, everything) said 31k with major climbs and that's what I prepared for. Turns out… not so much. We were starting out in Belorado, already at around 700 m elevation. Yes there were a couple of heart-racer hills but we got to 1100 m without too much trouble.

The scenery was sublime and occasionally poignant. Like outside Villafranca Montes de Oca where there is a stark plinth commemorating a mass grave of 300 people killed in the Spanish Civil War. The grave itself only discovered long decades after the fact.

Against this sadness, a little further down the track, at a crossroads surrounded by forest on all sides, was a man with a van and water, juice, fruit and a portable speaker playing a waltz. Surreal and superb. He is one of the many vendors who don't display a price. You pay what you can afford or want to give.

The rest of the day was spent with familiar faces catching up, walking by, being caught up to. At the top of one of the hills I finally met Kari. He's Finnish and my two walking companions had spoken to him at length before.

"Ah, Kari. I hear you were a Captain in the Finnish Army."

"Yes. I was a Ranger and a Regimental intelligence officer. I am still in the reserves."

And so began 20kms of two veterans talking about everything under the sun military-related, from current conflicts to the Battle of Britain, from training regimes to good and bad examples of leadership. Kari is such a well-read military historian it was a joy. He is also a man with a full head of long, unkempt grey hair. He admits he looks more like a hippie than a military reservist. He pointed to his hair, "I should explain, I play bass guitar and me and my friends from the 70s are getting the band back together."

At the next stop, the hamlet of San Juan de Ortega, we were joined by a man I'd first said hello to in St Jean. Alex, is a former German soldier now serving with the German Coast Guard (as close to navy as we were going to get). Over a drink, Kari, Alex and I wound-up, teased and generally laughed at each other's 'poor' choice of military Service. We swapped stories and fell into that, oh so comfortable inter-Service, international, NATO (now the Finns are members) banter. It was great.

Kari and Alex were staying in San Juan – in a monastery no less. And what a place - it's almost bigger than the village and was built (apparently) by Saint John of Ortega himself, with help from his friend and fellow saint (obviously, I mean you couldn't be a saint and hang around with non-saints, could you?) Domingo de la Calzada. Apparently these two built the monastery in the 1140s to aid pilgrims walking along the Way of Saint James. That sort of fact does send chills down my back. Nearly 900 years and here we are, still walking and still being helped. But all fortunes fluctuate and the monastery was abandoned in the nineteenth century, with local farmers using the church as a barn for hay. Nowadays, whilst the hamlet is still small, the increase in pilgrims has seen the former monastery undergo gradual restoration and a portion of it has been fitted out as an albergue with fifty beds.

We bade farewell to our companions of the day and Paddy, Popper and I carried on for another 7km to a 3-bed house we are sharing in Atapuerca. It was fantastic. And it had a fire. Thank goodness, as it was still bitterly cold. It also had a heated swimming pool, but we decided not to give it a go. Instead, we relaxed and reminisced.

Dinner was pizza in the 'Cantina', one of two restaurants in the tiny town, the other one having been… let's say, less than welcoming. Which was a shame as Atapuerca is a fascinating place. It's tiny, with a population in the hundreds, but it's also a UNESCO World Heritage Site. There's a massif above the town and as well as being the site of a battle in 1054, it was, in 1899, the place where some entrepreneurial types decided to build a railway to access a couple of quarries. The venture was not a success but it uncovered some caves which provided evidence of early human occupation. Bone fragments found in its Gran Dolina cavern turned out to be the oldest known evidence of hominid settlement in Western Europe and of hominid cannibalism anywhere in the world. You can't casually visit the sites, but you can get a tour through the Museum of Human Evolution in Burgos. Something I may well do in future years.

For now, we enjoyed the heat of the fire and the fact we could cook our own breakfast in the morning, making full use of the excellent kitchen and spacious dining room.

Steps walked: 46,146 (My biggest total on the Camino)
Camino distance travelled: 30.98kms
Total elevation ascents: 581m
Total descents: 399m

Day 14

April 19th 2024
Atapuerca - Burgos
Planned distance: 19km

Today was always planned to be 10km shorter than yesterday. We left later, which was good as it allowed the deep frost that we could see outside to lift a little. Setting off at 9am meant that the temperature was ideal, idyllic even, and the going (after the first mandatory hill / small mountain) was easy. The scenery, being that we were up at about 1000 metres, was panoramic and the twin villages of Cardeñuela Riopico and Orbaneja Riopico were as quaint as any we've seen… and yet, oh my goodness me, it was hard over the last 5km. Really hard. Not physically, but mentally. Perhaps it was the combination of 52kms over 2 days, or the seemingly never-ending walk along the banks of the Río Arlanzón into Burgos, a stretched out city where the old centre is at the far (west) end of the town, or the fact I picked up a bit of a head cold from the freezing chills yesterday, (paracetamol and orange juice will deal with it, so no biggie) but whatever the reason, I arrived into my apartment completely knackered. And still, a shower and a change of clothes makes everything right.

Dressed and back out we wandered about the city a little, had great food in the *Café Bar Alvaro* on *Calle Nuño Rasura* (seriously, the ultimate Spanish version of a classic Aussie dinner, Parmi and chips with two fried eggs). Ohhhh it was soooo good. As you will know by close observation, I am not a sports-dietician, but sometimes there's a lot to be said for carb loading and protein!

Between wandering about and eating, the three of us also visited Burgos Cathedral. As well as my non-dietician qualifications, you may have already gathered that I'm not a fan of organised religions, of any persuasion. No problem with people having their own beliefs and faith, but the organised bit, where men get much too involved with things, is not for me. However, religion was of course the reason for the Way existing and surviving for over a millennium, and still now each person who walks it has their own degree of faith or attachment to a particular denomination. Some are immersed, some aren't and some are somewhere in between. It matters not.

In my case, I can still appreciate the vast human ingenuity, effort, artistic creativity, time and resources that went into the Pyramids, or Christian cathedrals. In Burgos, the cathedral is immense. In every correct sense of that word. So impressive is it, that I would struggle to adequately describe the art, the iconography, the gold altars, silver crucifixes, carvings, windows, tapestries and vaulted cloisters. And so, I will defer to a conversation I had in the gift shop. (Bear with me, it is relevant).

I've mentioned Camille before. She is French, was walking the Camino on her own, but travelling in loose 'formation' with Tim, Deb, Bob and a few others. She had horrendous luck early on and suffered a horrible foot problem, yet with assistance from Tim she struggled on, and as the days went by the pain eased. Others helped, but mainly her continued journey was (in the same way as Popper's) down to her own grit and determination. We knew Camille was only walking to Burgos this time, as she had to get back to her life, and the way people drift in and out of focus on the Way it was doubtful any of us would get to say, "Cheerio".

Prior to going around the cathedral, I meandered around the gift shop. My wife likes religious gift shops. It's a long story but it's one of our quirks. I had been set the task of getting something from Santiago, but I thought I'd see if there was anything suitable here. There wasn't. But there was Camille, buying gifts for her family a couple of hours before she was due to leave for home. A greatly fortuitous encounter that allowed us to say goodbye. She asked if I'd been around the cathedral yet.

"Nope."

"You're in for an experience. I'm not really into religion, but I think it is the most incredible cathedral I have ever seen."

"What? More so than Notre Dame?"

This French lady nodded. That probably sums up the splendour of Burgos Cathedral better than I ever could.

Camile also gifted me one of the best interruptions to a conversation I've ever heard.

I was agreeing with her, "Yeah, I'm not into the whole religious thing either, but I do appreciate what can be done with centuries of—" I was going to say human ingenuity and artistic creativity…

Camille interrupted with, "Money and slaves, yeah. Definitely."

I laughed out loud and got, "Shooshed!" by the lady at the gift shop counter.

Whatever the reason or however it got built, Burgos Cathedral is stunning. As was the apartment I stayed in. My favourite place so far. The *Bella Vista Catedral-Apartamentos,* had, as its name suggests, a beautiful view of the cathedral from the small balcony set off the main lounge. Everything was new, having been recently refurbished and the apartment was a delight, equipped with everything you could possibly need. This was **not** doing the Camino hard. This was easy street.

Tomorrow would be even easier. A train trip. Oh, and almost getting arrested.

Steps walked: 37,216 (lots of them wandering around Burgos)
Camino distance travelled: 20.39kms
Total elevation ascents: 333m
Total descents: 423m

Day 15

April 20th 2024
Burgos - Astorga
Planned distance: 224km – by train

When planning this trip, we didn't think of doing the Camino in stages over a couple of years. We wanted to start in Saint-Jean and finish in Santiago, but to manage the distance in the time available, we had to 'lose' about 250km. So today, we would catch a train to Astorga, thereby cutting out the '*meseta*', literally the table flat lands.

Let's fast-forward to the afternoon and our train experience. We had a journey of 244km courtesy of Renfe, the Spanish train operator. Now… Spanish trains are GREAT. They are clean, fast and efficient. Spanish train stations are lovely, but Spanish train security is tight, for very obvious and tragically sad reasons. That means there is an airport-like security boarding system. Your bags are scanned. Unfortunately, no one had mentioned this and, I've since double-checked, it says nothing on the tickets nor in the station about what is and is not allowed. Or if it does, we three missed it.

Before we even got to the check-in part of the journey, we'd had a small incident. A customer using the vending machine had a can of coke explode on opening. They looked embarrassed and wandered away. We waited, but no cleaner seemed to be forthcoming. Popper got up and placed a couple of metal-legged stools either side of the large sticky puddle on the concourse, to deter someone from slipping in it. One Spanish security guard became very annoyed at this and shouted, a lot. From behind Popper, his mate approached quietly with his hand reaching for the baton he wore at his side. I discarded my backpack and started moving forward. What was I going to do? Probably get my head caved in with a baton, but I wasn't thinking that far ahead, however, all was resolved when the can buyer returned and explained what had happened. Calm descended.

Then our train's arrival was announced and we moved forward to the ticket desk and security screening area.

We three 'Norn Irish' lads had our backpacks pulled for additional security screening. *(Just cos you're paranoid doesn't mean they're not out to get ya!!).*

The charming security man started shouting very loudly and pointing at me and my kit. He was saying a word I didn't understand. Many words if I'm honest. I said, in Spanish, "I don't understand that. Can you say it in English?"

He replied at top volume, in Spanish, (and this is verbatim) "This is Spain. We speak Spanish here. Not English."

He kept shouting in rapid fire annoyance. I said, in Spanish, "I speak a little Spanish. I am speaking Spanish, but can you slow down please?"

He shouted more, stood up and pointed to a picture of a machete stuck to the side of his scanner. Next to it a diagram showing blades over 7.6cm (3") were banned. Then he gestured towards my backpack.

It finally dawned on me. I had a corkscrew/bottle opener/knife in my kit. You know the type of thing; it's usually called a waiter's friend. I fished it out and handed it over. He laboriously pulled out a ruler and measured the 5.6cm (2") blade. With a scowl, he handed it back. Paddy's similar gadget was also cleared. We were allowed to go on our way.

The next 'Cultural Ambassador to pilgrims in Spain' went back to his scanning machine. The lads said, as we settled down on the train, "I bet he's going in the book!"

Yes, yes he is, but more so as a cautionary tale for other train-jumping pilgrims. Be cautious of the Spanish train transport police, in Burgos at least. They seem to need more sleep, or a course in customer interactions, or some warm milk. Perhaps a hug?

With that encounter behind us, as we sped through the table-flat Spanish countryside at 247 kph, I focussed on the city we had left.

Burgos was beautiful. I wish we had been able to stop for a couple of days. I read about their amazing museums, including the Museum of the Book and the earlier mentioned, Human Evolution Museum with specimens of Europe's earliest hominin from Atapuerca. I could have spent days wandering their halls, but this was a rest day. We did go for a dander to find the castle. I had the map. We didn't find it. I am not in charge of 'tourist excursions' for the rest of the Camino and barred from having a map.

I left the city thinking that the digs I'd enjoyed, looking out at the cathedral, probably wouldn't be beaten on this trip. I was disproven in a single day!

The train arrived into Astorga at 17:38. We walked up (a hill) to Posada Real Casa de Tepa. We three had booked it as part of our 'rest day' criteria. Willing to spend a little more than our average €35-€50 per night, this one was €81. We thought we had booked a 'slightly better' hotel. We hadn't. Simply put, it's probably the best €81 for a room we're likely to spend on this trip or any other.

Tepa's House was the family home of the Tepa dynasty. It is, as best as I can describe it, a stately home. When Napoleon's forces staged through the city back in the day, Napoleon used it as his lodgings. We are sleeping in a house where Bonaparte slept. Well… if it's good enough for Napoleon, it's good enough for Craigyhill'ians.

You can stay in multi-person dorms on the Camino for €15 to €20 to €35, but sometimes it is worth spending a little more to stay encapsulated in history. We weren't expecting it and so it was even more astonishing. From the outside honesty bar set in the delightful gardens to the interior's reading rooms and lounges, it was a bit dreamlike. Dinner was equally sumptuous in the Restaurante Serrano, a local restaurant featuring fine Mediterranean cuisine and even finer wines. Expensive? Yes, much more than the standard pilgrim's menu, but sometimes you have to treat yourself. Paddy, Popper and I seem to implicitly agree that life is way too short not to be indulgent on occasion.

It was also an evening of reflection. Jumping ahead 250kms meant the Camino buddies we'd grown familiar seeing, would be lost to us. Tomorrow, we'd be in the company of others who had probably done the full walk across the Meseta. I wondered if it might make a difference. Turns out, it didn't. It simply meant we got a second set of Camino buddies. And we had the WhatsApp details of the former ones. Bonus! One tragedy though. No more Covinolas.

Tomorrow would be Astorga to Foncebadón. Estimated at 26km. And hills. Lots of big hills. Within the next two days we'd climb to the highest point on the Camino. We were looking forward to it.

Our evening ended sipping beers from the Tepa's honesty bar. Our un-confiscated bottle openers came in handy.

Steps walked: 11,583
Camino distance travelled: 0 – (and 224kms in real terms)
Total elevation ascents: 0m
Total descents: 0m
Arrests: 0

Day 16

April 21st 2024
Astorga - Foncebadón
Planned distance: 26kms

As I reflect on things now, this was my favourite day of the Camino. The weather, the terrain, the 'target' of the distant hills and the craic. All topped off with a destination that was a gem. But we didn't know any of that first thing in the morning. What we did know was that after the preceding evening's meal and wine, we were going to have a more leisurely start.

Deciding to have breakfast in 'Napoleon's old digs', we finally left Astorga at about nine'ish. Leaving the town we passed the impressive cathedral, (which we probably should have spent more time looking at considering it was designated a national monument in 1931) and the neighbouring Episcopal Palace, which we definitely should have spent more time looking at, given it was designed Antoni Gaudí. Yep, that Gaudí. It's one of only three buildings by him outside his native Catalonia. As I passed by, gazing up to its turrets and not knowing much about the *Catalan Modernisme* style of architecture, I thought it looked a bit like the Disney Castle. The view of this man-made wonder was quickly surpassed by snow-tinged mountain peaks towering up in the distance.

The day was spent trekking up a gentle incline, but as we pushed through the 'usual' stop on this stage, Rabanal del Camino, the gains in elevation began to increase sharply. Every step took us closer to those distant heights we had seen in the morning and especially one, that seemed to act like a beacon, marked with a slash of white across its slopes. Having started out looking up at them, by the time we had attained 1,442 metres, we were ever so slightly looking down on those nooks and crannies where the last remnants of snow still lingered.

It was mid-afternoon when we strolled into the minuscule village of Foncebadón. Population: (depending on when you conduct the census) eight or nine. Three of whom are children who go to Astorga for school. Takes them about half an hour to get there in a car. Took us about 6.5 hours to walk it. Again, the mind-blowing reality of how modern transport shrinks the world, usually invisible to us in our daily lives, was made starkly visible by the Camino.

The village is also home to a '9-month of the year' population who staff all the albergues, hostels and hotels. It is one of the smallest yet best equipped villages. The *El Trasqu Hostal's* store has everything a pilgrim could need, from spare laces to blister treatments, protein bars to cans of baked beans, as well as tons of souvenirs and guidebooks. It also has a bar, restaurant, an amazing dining room and its accommodation is where I am staying tonight. Proof, if needed, that whilst the House of Tepa, with its Napoleonic heritage, was fabulous, a €49 single room with a private shower in Foncebadón is more than sufficient. I loved the room, the village and the fact those distant, high mountains of the morning were now my neighbours, a mere valley away and almost level with my eye line.

Strangely though, bar one conversation Paddy had with a Mexican guy, the rest of the road was quiet and we saw few other pilgrims. I guess our delayed start meant the rest of the peregrinos coming out of Astorga were a couple of hours ahead of us. The lack of pilgrims allowed the three of us to walk the pre-noon hours in near silence, contemplating the road and the joy of the horizon.

As noon passed, we reminisced about the 'old days' in Northern Ireland. How the realities we had taken for granted whilst growing up, turned out to be *not* the norm. How we had discovered, as our older selves travelled abroad, that kids in New Zealand or America, England or Australia, hadn't grown up in the atmosphere and daily truths we had experienced. The sound of Army helicopters over-head, masked men marching in the streets, nightly news broadcasts on tea-time TV telling of bombings and shootings. How an empty car parked in the town centre meant trouble. How you became inured to the cursory searches conducted as you walked into shops and how discerning what 'religion' anyone and everyone was by the school they went to, or had gone to, or the place they worked, or even their name, was an unconscious 'skill' and why, to some, it mattered… And why, to all the people we called friends, it didn't.

We spoke about school, from our first days in primary school, to our last days at high school. We had shared them all. It seemed Popper and Paddy had kinder recollections of our high school than me. I detested the latter years of my school experience, but we had shared a common goal, in that none of the three of us could wait to get out of the place. We spoke of teachers and school-friends, the other kids in the town, the bigger, older kids, some of whom would get you a few beers from the off-licence if you caught them on a good day and some who were called tearaways, but in fact were borderline thugs and bullies who terrified you if you saw them walking down the street.

We spoke of the 'characters' in the town, the other families in 'our' streets, how we were suitably 'scared' and respectful of the adults, knowing (although none ever did) that they were within their rights to give you a clip round the ear for being cheeky and all our parents would have said was, "You must have deserved it."

We talked of the little three-legged dog that was a familiar sight in our estate. That estate, Craigyhill, apparently ahead of its time in design and layout, and where almost every street had an open green area, left clear and kept tended for kids to play. No council meddling and no 'Job's Worth' sign maker pleading for 'No Ball Games'.

And yes, we reflected on going out at sun-up in the holidays or weekends and getting back at dusk. We reflected on the scenery that had graced our every day, the mountains, rolling hills, plateaus and coastline that we had taken for granted, like we had taken the Army on our streets and the Troubles in our time.

As our walk neared its end and Foncebadón was in sight, we spoke of the heartache and pain of homesickness in those early days of being an émigré. The family occasions we had missed, the friends we had parted from and the sounds and rhythms of home we had lost. And finally, we talked of the amazing opportunities we had been afforded, the stunning places we'd been lucky enough to see and the fortunate new lives we had forged; reflecting on the reasons we had left and why we would be most unlikely to ever return for good.

***

Tomorrow is another 26+km day. including the *Cruz de Ferro*, the highest point on the Camino Francés between St Jean and Santiago. There will be lots more ascents and then it's all (allegedly) downhill to Ponferrada.

Steps walked: 38,328
Camino distance travelled: 26.04kms
Total elevation ascents: 692m
Total descents: 142m

Day 17

April 22nd 2024
Foncebadón - Ponferrada
Planned distance: 27kms

After the best breakfast I had on the Camino, massive shout-out to
Miguel and his team at El Trasgu, we set off uphill, but only a gentle
climb that brought us to the highest point between Saint-Jean-Pied-
de-Port and Santiago. The Iron Cross, or *Cruz de Ferro*.

There are lots of stories and traditions associated with the Cross,
but central to them is the leaving of a stone (or token) to represent
the shedding of burdens on the Way, or to remember those who are
no longer here. I chose the latter and left a stone and a small, wild
tree bud. One from Larne (my hometown), one from Leschenault
(where I live now). Together, they represent a lot of people who are
no longer here. My wife's family, my family, friends and comrades.
Paddy and Colin had their own moments. We also had a list, made
up of far too many names, of former classmates who have passed
away. Paddy read them out softly. We stood at 1,504 metres above sea
level and fell silent.

For the rest of the day, we would lose 1,000 metres of elevation.
Descending steep inclines and navigating extremely rough ground,
yet all the while surrounded by the most breathtaking scenery. The
Spanish wildflowers seemed to have come out just for us. Cascades
of yellows, clumps of purples, and strips of reds and whites, all
backed by a deep, luscious green.

These steep descents are probably worth a mention. We've done
a few of them now and yes, they are rough on the calves, but they

can also be treacherous due to the underfoot conditions. It gets slippery, not only when wet but with the loose shale and gravel. During these times, I use trekking poles, which leads on to a whole other topic of discussion in relation to a specific kit choice. Namely, sticks.

Some people have two trekking poles. Some have one. Some have a walking stick or a staff, some have nothing. It's okay. Do what you want. Personally, I have two trekking poles which I learnt to use properly to go up or down steep inclines. Yes, it turns out there is a proper way to use trekking poles – seriously – YouTube it.

On flat terrain, I carry them both in my left hand, unused. Occasionally I employ the right-hand stick as a walking stick. I'm not here to tell you what to do, but for me, walking up and down hills, especially down, is easier with both trekking poles in use. Paddy and Popper have staffs. Sticks with a hand loop of leather at the top and a metal tip on the end.

I say they have staffs. Popper has had one since St Jean. Paddy has, well… you know he left one behind and then the Camino gifted him the 'German' trekking poles. We never caught up to the women who left them behind, but somewhere between Logroño and Burgos, he'd managed to leave those poles on the trail. Apparently the Camino provides and so far there must have been a few pilgrims who needed staffs.

Now Paddy has a new staff. Again, dark wood, but with knobbly bits this time. Once more, if his beard was longer, he'd look like Gandalf! When we are leaving anywhere, our last question tends to be, "Paddy, where's your stick?" It may be the subtitle of the book.

The descents finally levelled out and we stopped for a quick drink in the village of Molinaseca, falling in with Babette, from the Netherlands, Andy from England, Hannah from Cork and Colin from Dublin. They've been walking in a loose company since StJPdP, with some others joining in Pamplona. Needless to say, on this first encounter, the Cork, Dublin and Larne mix told stories, shared the craic and generally got on like we were all long-lost distant cousins. Given the size of our wee island, we probably are. I hoped we'd run into them all again. There were more stories to hear and Andy and Babette might get a word in edgeways next time.

At the edge of the *Mesón Puente Romano* beer garden, I dipped my feet in the freezing Rio Merulo, as it sped under another Roman bridge. The bitter cold of the water was a welcome balm to feet that had, 'put in a shift'. But they weren't done.

The last 6km took us into Ponferrada. The town is dominated by the Templar Castle. Yes, *The*, not *A* – this is the original Templar Castle. I had a toy castle with knights and horses when I was a little boy. Hadn't thought about it in decades, but I'm pretty certain that toy castle was based on this actual one. It's like it was designed by a child given the brief of, "Make a castle."

It looks like you imagine a castle should look. Round towers, drawbridge, moat, more towers and flags. It's great! Only thing missing is a dragon.

And so, the day drew to a close, but not before a bit of modern technology raised our spirits beyond all manner of heights achieved or castle fortresses observed.

I sat in an ice cream shop and watched on my phone, Larne playing Linfield in the Northern Irish Football League's penultimate round of games. A single point for Larne would win back-to-back league titles. Larne players straining every sinew, their red and white strips on the deep, luscious green turf of Windsor Park, NI. The result was a draw. Good enough! Brilliant in fact. After that excitement it was time to sleep. The next two days were going to be a test. Lots of walking, and lots of reclaiming the height we lost today.

Steps walked: 40,565
Camino distance travelled: 27.35kms
Highest Elevation: 1,509m
Total elevation ascents: 388m
Total descents: 1,261m

Day 18

April 23rd 2024
Ponferrada - Villafranca del Bierzo
Planned distance: 26kms

Ah we all know a big, big day is coming tomorrow for today was far too pleasant a meander up and down through stunning countryside and quaint villages. Well, it was once we got out of Ponferrada.

Somewhat ironically, for the home of the original Templar Knights and their renowned hospitality for pilgrims, it seemed, last night anyway, that the town was a tad more 'hostility' than hospitality. I thought it was probably my wrong impression after a hard day, but turns out Popper and Paddy had similar experiences. All the staff in the hotels or cafés, bar one, had been very glum. The same was true in the morning, so we headed off early and found much more welcoming faces about 5k down the road.

For a while I pondered again on how this trip, unlike anything I've done before (a different town every day at 'ground level') reveals the character of regions, cities, towns and villages in sharp relief. The immediate sense of a place, passers-by greeting you, or dropping their eyes, or staring blank and resolutely ahead. Customer service venues offering warm welcomes or surly grunts. And then I stopped pondering and drew breath at the mountains behind us (those snowy peaks we had reached and then descended down over the last two days) and those ahead, which bar our way to Santiago. In between, rolling hills of vineyards and secluded villages. I walked the rest of the day with a grin on my face. Although the Cornetto XXL ice cream I had after lunch in Cacabelos also contributed to the feeling of joy and exuberance – (seriously, it was massive). The sugar rush kept me meandering along for the rest of the afternoon.

On arrival at Villafranca, I was greeted by the on-duty person at my digs, Juan. Friendly and engaging, he couldn't have made me feel more welcome. I dropped my kit and carried on into the square to meet up with Paddy and Popper. We were soon joined by Hannah and Colin (Dublin-Colin) from last night. More craic ensued and Colin shared the tale of his first day on the Camino Francés. He, like us, had chosen to do Route Napoleon in a single day. He though, did it in March, before it's official 2024 opening and he did it alone, with only his own will to drive him forward. Except, he did get company. A collie dog, who he'd nickname, Jean, followed him out of StJPdP (with no encouragement). The dog stayed with him for over 25kms until it saw Colin safely into Roncesvalles. Eventually, after calls back to Saint-Jean, the owner was identified and they came to pick their dog up. *Colin and the Collie Dog*. I see a book deal?

As the evening progressed, Paddy, Popper and I chatted about the upcoming days. According to the Camino App, tomorrow was:

The last day in Castile and León and one of the toughest throughout the pilgrimage, entering Galicia through the narrow valley of the river Valcarce and the ascent to the legendary O Cebreiro mountain pass.

The problem with a day like that was Popper's foot had been causing him increasing problems and he needed to rest it. He and Paddy settled on a plan of attack. I decided that I would try to press on to O Cebreiro. What's the O stand for? Oh, that's high up and far away.

Steps walked: 38,825
Camino distance travelled: 25.92kms
Total elevation ascents: 744m
Total descents: 757m

Day 19

April 24th 2024
Villafranca del Bierzo – O Cebreiro
Planned distance: 29kms

Okay, the headline is, *today was brutal at times but always rewarding*.

We know we've been blessed with an unusually warm and dry April to date, but alas the forecast is set to change. Today, as I set off from the hill town of Villafranca at 08:00, it was barely one degree Celsius. The wind was cutting and the sun nowhere near high enough to get a look down into the deep valley which the Camino was tracking. It took an hour and a half before the valley sides relaxed and the sun made a welcome appearance. Even with the relatively quick pace I was doing, I was still freezing. Yet, in the next town, Trabadelo, the strange ability of the Camino to provide occurred again. A small doorway, a sign saying, 'Food, drink - Come in' and the most welcoming couple, Adrian and Dianna. They made the best tea and toast and provided a fire to thaw beside. A real fire. Logs and coal and flames. I was sooooo grateful. We shall return to the fireside in a moment, but first…

This was the second Dianna I'd met that morning. In Villafranca, I'd shared breakfast with San Diego natives, Derrick and his mum, Dianna. They are walking the Camino together and their close bond and gentle conversation reminded me of how my mum and I had been. I glanced across to the empty chair at the breakfast table for four and felt a serene calmness.

Later, we'd be joined by Pierre from Switzerland, before all four of us, breakfast done, set off into the freezing morning.

And here I was now, warming up and being offered tea and toast. The Camino provides! And I wasn't the only one being provided for. Sitting at the long dining table in Adrian and Dianna's were two young women. Belen, from Madrid and Tessa from Chicago. They had become casual walking buddies, separating and joining like leaves borne on currents. For now, they greeted me like a life-long friend. After the mandatory name, where are you from, etc… introductions, Tessa said, "Oh, you're one of the Irish guys, schoolfriends, you're all doing this together. One of you is writing about it!"

"Uh, umm, yeah. How on earth do you know that?"

"We were talking about you last night in the albergue."

"Wow! Fame at last!"

We five chatted happily about the cold morning and the fun of the Camino for both pilgrims and hosts. As usual, Belen, Dianna and Adrian all spoke wonderful English. We shared more rounds of tea and toast and then it was time for Tessa and Belen to move on. As Tessa stood she involuntarily yelped in pain. Belen said that her friend was suffering with a bad blister.

Dianna motioned for het to sit back down by the fireside and she would take a look at it. Thinking I might be able to help, I reached into my pack and pulled out my tiny first aid kit. Looking up I saw Adrian motion that it was okay. He walked to a cupboard and lifted out a paramedic's backpack. It was huge. Dianna had already fished out a pair of surgical gloves from another drawer.

She said by way of explanation, "I used to be a nurse."

Belen and I tried not to show any trace of concern on our faces, but it was hard not to react when Tessa removed her sock. Even the former nurse said, "Oh!"

If we'd been anywhere else, I'm sure Tessa would have been calling a taxi. As it was, Dianna expertly treated and dressed the ball and heel of Tessa's foot as well as strapping her ankle. I was beginning to grasp just how the Camino provides.

Tessa and Belen gave hugs all round and set off on their way. I finished my tea and Adrian insisted that four euros was more than enough for the sustenance provided. It wasn't, but it was all he would take. He and Dianna came to the door to bid me farewell.

The rest of my day was spent in various conversations with passing pilgrims. Some walked alongside for an hour or so, some for a few minutes. Luca, Lauren and, as the day drew to a steep and testing end, Pierre again. Each had their own story, each their own reasons for being on the Camino. The diversity and range probably best summed up by comparing just two: Lauren, Canadian, 35, thinking about the Camino when she was leant the book, *Two Steps Forward* written by Anne Buist and Graeme Simsion. It gave her the final push to come on the Way. She was a happy, chatty, confident *Swiftie,* who was walking the Camino on her own terms, determined to complete the challenge. After Santiago she was considering pressing on to Fisterra, considered in the middle ages to be the end of the world.

In contrast, Pierre, 77, a proud grandfather who, after six years of walking sections annually, is entering the final week of a Camino that has stretched from his home in Switzerland through to Santiago, some 2000+kms.

When Lauren found out that I knew (or at least am Facebook friends with) Anne and Graeme, she was delighted. Personally, I was delighted that she and I had met on the approaches to La Faba. The road through the village of Las Herrerias is as gorgeous as you could wish for, the village idyllic, the Rio das Lamas running alongside provides a gentle trickle of calm and serenity. It is nature's way of getting you prepared for what is coming. A couple of kilometres further and the climb, through a fern-lined gorge towards La Faba is punishing. I met Lauren at the foot of it and together we encouraged each other to make the next bend, the next tree, the next patch of sunlight. Any small goal to keep ourselves going. At the top, Lauren was stopping in the local albergue. I wandered on, found a café, got something to eat, checked my feet and got ready to go again.

The next climb up to La Laguna de Castilla was tough, but not as bad as La Faba. Again, at the top there was a café. Sitting in the sun enjoying a beer were some French, a Canadian, a couple of Spaniards, including Luca, and Pierre. I wasn't sure how or when he had passed me; but here he was! I was invited to join them.

Most of the company were stopping in La Laguna, but like me, Pierre and Luca were determined to press on to O Cebreiro. After a couple of drinks, we gathered ourselves and set off on the final climb of just over 2k. It doesn't sound far, but by now we had walked 27k and were facing another 140m climb. We three, walking at our own pace, threaded our way up, at one point crossing the border from Castile and León into Galicia; Celtic Spain. Only 161km to Santiago.

The reward for the effort was revealed on the last rise up to the O Cebreiro mountain pass. The white clouds thinned, revealing a bright blue Galician sky and allowing the sun to light up the *Sierra dos Ancares* and the distant rolling hills that form part of the *Montes de León* and the *Macizo Galaico*. It was breath taking.

Pierre and I strode up the final rise together and into O Cebreiro. Later we'd bump into each other at dinner. During the meal he took a quick call from his granddaughter. I didn't understand the rapid French conversation, but I didn't have to. The closeness of the bond was more than evident in the tones of a grandfather's affection.

OC is a quaint little place, full of touristy trinkets, a couple of restaurants and beautiful buildings in the style of palloza houses, oval with low walls and straw roofs. No wonder the place is a UNESCO World Heritage Site.

Tomorrow - OC to Triacastela. Planned distance: 21km and another couple of big peaks to get over. But also, if I can get my act together, at the end of the day I will rejoin Paddy and Popper.

Steps walked: 42,286
Camino distance travelled: 29.95kms
Total elevation ascents: 1,484m
Total descents: 691m

Day 20

April 25th 2024
O Cebreiro – Triacastela
Planned distance: 22kms

Today is Anzac Day.

A special day in Australia's calendar. It marks the landings in 1915 by British and Commonwealth (the Empire as it was then) forces along with their French and other allies. They were opposed by the Turkish troops of the Ottoman Empire, defending their home soil.

It was far from a military victory for the Australians.

The number of ANZAC casualties was less than other nations fighting on that peninsula and Australia would lose far greater numbers in the mud and mire of the Western Front.

However, despite all this, Gallipoli was the first time Australia had fought in open warfare as an independent country. The sacrifice of so many (as a percentage of the fledgling nation's population) became a symbol of Australian nationhood. And so, every April, we commemorate the ANZACs of Gallipoli and all those other men and women, from every race, creed and home country who have called Australia home, fell in service for her and paid the ultimate price to grant me and all my fellow Australians the freedoms we enjoy. As I walked out of the village of O Cebreiro, the dawn was breaking. It was easy to recall the line from Laurence Binyon's poem, The Fallen, *'And in the morning… we will remember them.'*

***

Today's Camino was sponsored by Ibuprofen and Voltaren.

I may have hurt my right leg a few days ago. I slipped on the loose stones on top of the hill that supported the Iron Cross and over-extended my right ankle. Nothing to it, walk it off, 'She'll be right,' type of thing.

Woke this morning and sure enough all was well. Feeling happy and quite proud of my little body's recovery skills, I exited my digs into a bitterly cold day, had breakfast in a warm café, shared a quick cup of tea in the company of Belen and others, then set off. About 5km in, Karma reached out and applied a branding-iron to my leg. Well, I imagine that's what it might feel like. I pulled up quite quickly and took a minute. One protein bar, some water and two painkillers later, I set off again.

Limping through the next 10km, I kept up a decent regime of self-medicating with a mix of painkillers and anti-inflammatory tablets. By 15km it was all okay, or I had numbed it into submission. What was it? No idea. Maybe tendonitis, maybe a nerve. Whatever it was, it didn't come back. Lucky me.

Today was also extremely cold and even whilst climbing up outrageously severe slopes to reach the *Alto do Poio's* height of 1335 metres, I was still shivering. The sun made a brief appearance and I was glad for it, but even more grateful that the predicted rain held off, save for a couple of light spits. All in all, you'd be forgiven for thinking, *What a miserable day. What a miserable Camino.* But you couldn't be further from the truth. It was a glorious day.

Walking insulated from others on the road, enclosed in a damp bubble of introspection, I alternated between listening to my music and more often, listening to birdsong.

Tiny hamlets and farms popped up more regularly and photos might do justice to the general feel of them, but can't capture the aroma of the many, many cows about the place. When I was a boy, back in Larne, we used to walk up by a farm in a place called

McCleary's loanen. (Although for reasons I am not quite sure of, the name of the place seems to be a source of argument back home… It was definitely McCleary's to me and my mates.) Anyway, the smells of today whisked me back there. Having to wait for the cows to be moved into new pastures was also an experience I haven't had for decades. It was fun having to stop and watch time (and cows) pass unhurriedly. A chestnut tree in Ramil, not far from the bovine road-block, is billed as being over 800 years old. The sign explaining its heritage prompts the reader to ask what sights it has seen. A lot of cows was the answer I came up with.

On arriving into Triacastela, I found my digs at the Complexo Xacobeo Albergue & Pensión. The single room was in what used to be a prison for inebriated pilgrims or those who had fallen foul of some other un-pilgrim-like misdemeanour. Thankfully, the building has seen some major renovations since and the room was cocoon-like-warm, comfortable, clean and yet again, equipped with a shower that was deliciously hot and powerful enough to mean it needed to be turned down. Seriously, what is it with Spanish plumbers!!

After sorting me and my kit, I meandered down to meet Paddy and Popper. Reunited, we headed out for a meal of carb loading and drinks in the adjacent Complexo Xacobeo restaurant.

The dining area was split into three, with tables near the bar, some in the next room and then, down a hall and round a corner, a larger space. In each section were familiar faces. Andy from Villafranca, a Korean couple I had met first in Foncebadón, the Canadians, French and Spanish from La Laguna and, at the table one over from where we eventually got shown to sit, Lauren from that slog up to La Faba. In the middle of a crowded restaurant of pilgrims she jumped up and gave me a hug. No one batted an eye.

As Paddy, Popper and I settled down to another excellent meal, we reflected on some sad news from back home. Michael, due to be joining us this week, had broken his foot. Bad as it was, it could have been a lot worse had he done it over here, on the way to Santiago.

We were sad, but of course what we actually did was take the mickey out of him and his plastic boot before calling it a night. There haven't been too many late nights pulled on the trip so far, and tonight was another early call. I was knackered. The bitter cold of the day had worn me out and I didn't fancy being an inebriated pilgrim, even if my room was historically capable of coping.

Tomorrow will take us from Triacastela to Sarria. The planned distance had been estimated at 18k, but now it'll be 25km along the more picturesque route. The forecast is rain. It won't dampen our spirits. Especially mine. I have good reason to be happy tomorrow.

Steps walked: 36,080
Camino distance travelled: 22.01kms
Total elevation ascents: 421m
Total descents: 1,047m

Day 21

April 26th 2024
Triacastela – Sarria
Planned distance: 25kms

It's my birthday! The day began with a plethora of very kind birthday wishes on social media from family and friends and all those who had been following my posts about doing the Camino. I was humbled. As I was when meeting up with Popper and Paddy at the start of today's walk and they serenaded me with a very tuneful rendition of, 'Happy Birthday'. Not sure what the rest of the pilgrims made of it but I was not concerned. Seeing 'them two eejits' standing at the fork in the road where one way is to Sarria (18kms) and the other way is to Sarria (25kms) is an image that will live long in my memory (and for many more birthdays I hope).

I really did appreciate every good wish I received. It was a great start to the day and made me feel extremely lucky to be able to spend my birthday with some of my friends (and we'd be meeting another one later). Nonetheless, I wouldn't be spending it with my best friend, Jacki. My being on the Camino was only possible because of her support and commitment over our years together. We've been married almost half our lives. She makes me a better person and encourages me to go off on wild notions of wandering across Spain for the fun of it. She is my sounding board, my advisor, my harshest critic and my greatest strength. She is also excruciatingly truthful. As we set off today, I recalled her response to my suggestion of doing the Camino together… "No. God No! Why would we do that?"

However, here I was, and with my two companions we decided not to go the short way (18k) to Sarria but rather take the 25km route. Allegedly, the 25kms was meant to be flatter (it was not) and prettier (it was). All in all,… a good choice. If you find yourself in Triacastela at the fork in the Avenue Camilo Jose Cela, then go right, down the small hill. It's worth it.

After about 4km I felt we'd been transported back to the 17th century. The hamlets, if they could even be called that, comprised of one or two houses built of tightly stacked slate, with musket slots in the walls. Quiet rivers and streams gurgled past unseen. The sound of the water accompanied by the occasional cockerel crow or cows lowing. Sudden choruses of gentle, twittering birdsong, amidst the scent of trees, then a brief light shower and that amazing earthy smell called petrichor.

Not a car, not a shop. And yet still, smoke twirling up from a chimney, evidence of occupancy in a world so alien to this time. Beautiful, sad and strangely poignant.

We walked on, along the course of now visible waterways and came down into Samos. Home to one of the most magnificent monasteries on the Camino Francés. Dating back to the 6th century it is an awe-inspiring site, from the first glimpses we caught looking down from the high ground, to eventually looking up at it from the small bridge crossing the Rio Sarria in Samos itself.

We decided to stop for lunch and were joined by two cyclists. Now… cyclists on the Camino trail is a whole different book. And quite a tetchy subject sometimes. They tend to belt along, occasionally not sure what side of the track to belt along on. Being very quick and often very silent, they can be nearly on top of pilgrims before yelling out a warning. I've seen four near accidents so far. It's not helped by the fact many pedestrian pilgrims are also unsure about what side of the track to walk on, or are simply used to the road being completely unused by traffic and so they meander left, right and centre. Personally, over the course of the last few weeks, I could have throttled one or two of the cyclists who appeared out of no-where and made me jump… had I been able to catch them. Seriously folks, fit a bell. And use it.

By the nature of the differences in speed, we hadn't spent much time conversing with any of them, but we had spoken to one or two during stops and they always seemed pleasant folk. Marco and Anastazja, who joined us this lunchtime were no exception to that. Yet again, trying to greet them in Spanish was a non-starter as both spoke perfect English. Mind you, they had good reason to.

Marco is Italian, but used to live near Bath in England. He speaks flawless English, supports Liverpool Football Club and his favourite band is Stiff Little Fingers. Basically, he is Italian, but a bit British on the inside with (and I realise I may be biased) excellent taste in foot-ball and music!

Anastazja is from Poland. She also introduced herself in perfect English because she was raised in Peterborough, England, graduated from Bristol Uni and then decided to move back to Kraków to better immerse herself in her Polish culture. Turns out that when I men-tioned I used to live in a small Cambridgeshire village near Peterborough, we had a lot of shared places to chat about.

After a while, they set off on their speedy transports and Paddy, Popper and I walked on to the slower rhythm of gently tapping walk-ing staffs and trekking poles. We were a fair bit up the road when we noticed the gentle rhythm of the tapping wasn't as loud as it should have been.

"Hey, Paddy. Where's your stick?"

And yet again, the Camino had provided. I hope whoever picked it up loved it, cos it was a properly nice, dark wood staff.

"Do you want to stop and buy another one at the next stop?" Popper and I enquired.

"Nah. I'm over it. I'll be fine without one."

We wandered on, through pastureland and along back roads, all the while serenaded by birdsong and the soft patter of a calming rain.

Later, we stumbled upon a tucked away café. With its welcoming flags and eclectic mix of garden ornaments and paraphernalia it seemed quite quirky. As we walked down the slope into the small, concreted seating area, the quirkiness became a little less quirky and more, "Uh-oh." The agreed feeling was that if a couple of kids walked out playing duelling banjos, it wouldn't have been a surprise. By that time though, we'd been greeted by the hosts. We had a swift drink, pressed money into their hands... and pressed on. Thankful.

By the end of a long day, the entry into Sarria was quite drawn out. Our accommodation for the night was at the far end of town, but worth it as we'd all be staying together in a 5-bed apartment. I say all, for we were to be joined by the fourth of our troop, but as we knew already, not the fifth. We will now be the Four Amigos. C'est la vie. But oh, the craic was mighty.

Mark, our new arrival brought us Norn Irish Tayto cheese and onion crisps and Larne Football Club baseball hats. We went to a supermarket and stocked up on food. And alcohol. As we wandered around the aisles, I was greeted by a woman customer who said, "Hola, how was your day?" like I was a local. I took a double take. She had served us breakfast in Triacastela that morning. Her home is in Sarria and the hotel she works in is a short commute by car. I was again reminded of how modern transport makes such a mockery of distances.

And it certainly does. Mark had set off from Larne that day, driven to Dublin, flown to Spain and bussed it to Sarria. Now here we were, the four of us, sharing an apartment, 'ould' songs and older stories. As they say in Norn Iron, "Sure, where would you get it?"

Having introduced Paddy and Popper earlier, I guess I should say a word or two about Mark. He is my closest friend since childhood (pram-hood even, as we apparently first met whilst in them). We lived three doors from each other until I left to join up. His parents were de-facto 'Auntie' and 'Uncle' to me as mine were to him. Always taller than me, (who isn't) he and I decided at 4-years-old to swap clothes and houses, certain our mums wouldn't notice. I think they played along until tea-time and then sent us packing.

Our childhood record of 'important' days includes photos of us together. He was beside me when we found out we had both failed a school exam we'd been sure of passing. That particular day, Friday 13th August 1982, altered my life's trajectory. Mark had gone on to get an apprenticeship, staying in Larne and becoming a welder. He later travelled quite a bit with that skill, to South Korea and then to England. In the late 80s and early 90s we both lived in East Anglia, a few town's distance from one another. Again, we have photos of that time; both much younger, me much thinner. As for Mark, he doesn't seem to have changed a bit from those days, thanks to him being a keen cyclist and working at his fitness. He'd wanted to join us for the whole Camino adventure, but work meant he could only squeeze in the last stretch from Sarria to Santiago. Perhaps he'll do the rest in stages like so many we've met on the road.

With our shared friendship stretching back six decades, it was good to see him in company with Paddy and Popper. Adding Mark's sharp sense of humour into the mix, we spent the evening laughing about the misadventures of our youth, how Michael and Gerry had also been constants during those days and how their humour was equally vital and at times, withering, in the way you need your friends to be. It was a good evening, to top off a good day, in the midst of a great adventure.

Happy birthday to me!

And now to tomorrow. Sarria to Portomarín. Planned distance: 22kms. Hangover cure required: probably.

Happy days!

Steps walked: 38,542
Camino distance travelled: 25.70kms
Total elevation ascents: 775m
Total descents: 988m

Day 22

April 27th 2024
Sarria - Portomarín
Planned distance: 24kms

I learnt a new Spanish word today: *Nieve*. It means: Snow.

Yep, snow. After two weeks of blazing sun and one week of cold mornings with bright afternoons, today we got snow. Quite a lot of it. Then freezing rain. Oh, it was chilly. But what a laugh. I messaged home to Australia to say, "It's snowing," to which I got the reply, "Is that meant to happen in Spain?" Apparently so.

I did feel a bit sorry for Mark. He's put up with a terrible winter back in NI and, reading the progress reports of us in the sweltering sun in Spain, he flew out to what he had hoped would be balmy conditions. Instead, he gets this. Or perhaps he brought it with him?

Thankfully the Camino provided, in the shape of a cafe with warming drinks, even if we all had to stand outside in an undercover garden area. A small note here; when I say all, I mean a lot of all. There is such an increase in the number of walkers on the Way, now we have passed Sarria. The reason is that Sarria to Santiago is the minimum distance needed for walkers to complete in order to get the Compostella. From the days of us seeing a handful of fellow pilgrims on the road, we were now wading through tens, and occasionally, as at this first stop, nearer to fifty or more.

The weather was bizarre, but the chats between the four of us were lively and the time went by in good humour. We even ran into a couple of other Northern Irish walkers, the first of quite a few we'd meet over the next days. Two women from Coleraine and a couple of lads from Belfast. All of us agreed that, "Sure, it's just a typical summer's day back home."

Later on, with the snow turning to sleet, we came up on another knot of walkers. Most were walking, heads bowed against the gusting wind, but one of the figures was striding along, unconcerned by the conditions. I pushed the hood of my poncho back and called out, "Tessa?"

And yet again the Camino surprised me. We'd been in each other's company for fleeting moments a few days ago, yet this young woman sprinted back and gave me a hug like I was a long-lost family member. We fell into stride alongside each other and fell back into a comfortable conversation. I knew already that Tessa was originally from Chicago, but now I learnt that she'd lived in Arizona, travelled extensively in South and Central America as well as Europe and had been wanting to do the Camino for a few years. Not bad for someone who's only 20!

She is one of life's optimists, happy and always smiling, albeit she too was freezing. We chatted amiably and then paused as a herd of slow-moving cows plodded past. Although our conversation had ranged far and wide, and Tessa had a vast knowledge of the countries she'd been to, neither of us knew the first thing about livestock. We hadn't a clue what breed they were, but we decided we liked them. Waiting for them to mosey on out of the way, we also discovered that we knew little about the ferns growing on the verges, but we liked them too. A couple of hours later, I stopped off for a drink with my companions and Tessa walked on. A perfect snapshot of why this Camino is so fascinating. Snippets of meetings and conversations that make the days, be they sunny or snowy, fly past.

We eventually got to Portomarín, after a couple of treacherously wet and dangerous descents through broken stones and heavy mud. The bridge over the Miño River is beautifully situated and the steep flight of steps up into the town dramatically poignant. I was in a small and cheap apartment over a supermarket, The others in a multi-bed apartment just down the road. They had decided to go to the evening service in the very square Church of St. Nicholas. I decided that I'd get sorted and pop down to the supermarket for some food. On entering the apartment, I realised I didn't have to. Shown in by the lady who runs the complex, she gave me a quick tour and said that everything in the kitchen was for my use, before bidding me a good stay. There was enough food, snacks and drinks to feed a small army of pilgrims.

The apartment was immaculate and that's not hyperbole. It was sparkling, and made to feel like a home away from home. Whoever 'dressed' this place on a daily basis was exceptional at their job, and yes, the shower was amazing. Without question, this was the most welcoming and best equipped accommodation I stayed in throughout my entire Camino. Obviously, Napoleon's digs were the most interesting and 'plushest' but the *Alojamientos con encanto Ruliña* in Portomarín was a delight. Apparently the lads' accommodation was equally as good.

When the four of us met up for dinner, it was FREEZING. A bitter frost and a cutting wind had the town hunkering down. I was in shorts, a t-shirt and a fleece. Thankfully Portomarín had touristy shops selling touristy trinkets. And heavy jumpers. And the ugliest pair of black and dayglo yellow trim gloves you have ever seen, but I didn't care. They were mine now. I loved them instantly for the warmth they bestowed and ignored the fact they had shell motifs and 'The Camino' plastered over them in gaudy fonts. I am ready to brave tomorrow. The weather forecast is for a low of 3°C, and a high of 12°C. Brrrr.

Steps walked: 37,147
Camino distance travelled: 24.48kms
Total elevation ascents: 662m
Total descents: 697m

Day 23

April 28th 2024

Portomarín – Palais de Rei

Planned distance: 25kms – (But the guidebook was wrong)

A long day, which seemed to go on quite a bit, mainly due to the fact we thought we were looking at 25k and it was nearer 30. That extra 5k, well okay, 3 and a bit, is a test when you are at the end of a day and thinking the goal is around the next corner. Still, the terrain was interesting, a few more climbs, a few more descents, but no snow, although a smattering of hailstones kept us, 'honest'. Most of the extra distance was probably due to another fork in the road as we were leaving Portomarín. The Camino splits and you can take the 'complementary route' or the 'historical route'. We opted for the latter and branched left out of the town. The land rises up and up until it offers views over distant rolling hills, topped off, on this day, by scudding clouds and glimpses of aquamarine blue skies. Some of the climb was steep, but by now I guess we're used to it. In the afternoon the sun finally stretched itself to burn off a bigger gap in the clouds and I saw my shadow for the first time in a while.

The highlight of the day was saved for the end. After we arrived into Palais de Rei, I found my accommodation, the lads found theirs and Karma found all of us. My room was, for the first time on the trip, filthy. I decided that tonight, I'd be sleeping in my permethrin treated, bed-bug repellent, liner. The shower was a tub with a tap suspended over it and the floor was sticky. But it was warm. The lads in comparison had one radiator that didn't work that well, but at least their digs were clean. Yet this was one of the best nights on the

Camino. Wandering out through the streets of Palais de Rei we stumbled upon a pasta restaurant called, Pasta. We squeezed in, literally. The place has an upstairs apparently, though we never saw it as the few tables up there were occupied, so we took our place at the tiny, narrow counter. Well, we did eventually after some other folks had left. Initially we had to sit on the windowsill. All of which sounds terrible, but it wasn't. Whilst on the sill, we could still get a drink and order our food. Alas, again, no need for Spanish.

Pasta is owned by an English guy called, Chris and his wife, Jacqueline who comes from County Tyrone, Northern Ireland. She even had Punjana and Barry's tea bags on display, which if you are from either side of the Irish border, is a big deal. Yet Jacqueline's wasn't the only familiar sounding accent in the place.

As we manoeuvred into the small downstairs bar area, the four women who were ahead of us in the queue for a table were also speaking 'properly'. They hailed from Newry, County Down, and were on their last section of the Camino after starting back in 2018 (losing two years to Covid). Following ten minutes of playing 'who's who' it turns out that yes, we knew people they knew and vice versa. Oh, when I write this it makes Northern Ireland sound so small and interwoven. Like its some back-of-the-woods place where everyone knows someone, who knows someone who knows you. And the truth is, it is and they do!

A while later, the two Coleraine women we met yesterday, Ali and Gillian, came down from the restaurant itself. They both had a laugh about how our local football team had beaten theirs, 5-0 last night and reckoned they'd mention it before we did. And so, in a perfect wee pasta restaurant in Galicia, Spain, eleven Northern Irish natives talked at length and at speed, no doubt confusing the other waiting diners with just what sort of language these almost dozen folk were speaking. I know some English speakers who would have had a hard time keeping up, but goodness knows how the French and the Dutch that were also in there coped, let alone the two Americans who popped their head in the door to be told the place was full and they had no chance of a table. I think they may have thought they had a lucky escape!

If they did think that, they'd have been wrong, for the food was excellent. Garlic bread, padron peppers and Italian meatballs for starters and then all four of us decided the meat lasagna looked fantastic. It was. Yet more than the food and the craic was the fact that here in this little corner of a small Spanish town, Chris and his wife, Jacqueline have made a life for themselves doing exactly what they want. Good for them!

And so, to tomorrow. The Monday that kicks off our last week. A long-distance day, estimated by the guide at 30kms (but who knows). Lots of ascents and descents (kinda used to that now). Weather is better, hopefully, with no precipitation forecast (but who knows) yet chilly, so we will walk quickly and talk faster.

Steps walked: 39,169
Camino distance travelled: 28.95kms
Total elevation ascents: 1,445m
Total descents: 1,265m

Day 24

April 29th 2024
Palais de Rei – Arzúa
Planned distance: 29kms

We knew today was apparently going to be a big one, but yesterday had seen us ascend and descend a lot, so we figured today wouldn't be so bad. Assumptions can be a complete pain in the... foot.

Where yesterday the slopes had been mostly gentle curves, today, despite being half of the total ascent and descent heights of yesterday, the climbs were almost a constant up and down and up and down... and up and down. However, the weather forecast was spot on. No rain, sun in the late morning and afternoon. But because of the hills, it seemed to drag a little. We walked through numerous small villages and a couple of big towns but for the majority of the day the scenery was curtailed by high ravines on the descents and fairly high hedges or bland looking fields on the ascents. Still, there were the occasional highlights, rivers, bridges and finally, open vistas out to distant horizons to contemplate.

Also, more Norn Irish. David and Ivan, amiable and interesting, they were keen hillwalkers from Belfast, who we'd fleetingly met a few days earlier. We fell into easy conversation about the Camino, their training regime in the Mourne Mountains and how, as we neared Santiago, the numbers on the Way increased exponentially.

Interspersed with them, Sue from Vancouver was power-walking her way through the day with ease. We chatted about Canada, jobs (she's a retired nurse), our spouses, kids and grandchildren. Parting at the biggest town of the day I walked on with my companions and bumped into others we have met previously, Pierre, Luca, Diana and her son Derrick. Also new folks, like Andrea, who similar to Derrick, was walking with her mum, Blanca. Andrea had an infectious enthusiasm which warmed the bitter cold of the day and made anyone within her radius happier. As before, it struck me that it's like walking down a familiar high street with old friends and neighbours passing by. Quite surreal really.

The day, as well as being full of up and down terrain, was also a day of alternative routes. Paddy, Mark, Popper and I were, as usual, spread out along the road. There was a lot of WhatsApp'ing with instructions to go right, or left. Obviously, coming out of Melide, one of the bigger towns on the Camino, the phone signal was so bad that we ended up going our own ways. Eventually meeting up again at one point or another, invariably a bar of some description!

One definite highlight, early on in the day, was the food stop at the *Casa de los Somoza* in O Leboreiro. Superb food and lots of it, plus a stunning garden adjacent to the main restaurant, but my happiness was peaked as I walked up to the entrance of the place. Leaning against a wall having a cigarette, was a man who like me had been freezing in Portomarín. How do I know? Well, he too had a pair of the ugliest gloves in Christendom. I nodded to him, glanced at his gloves and held up my hand. He nodded sagely, like a wizard greeting a fellow mage, knowing that only they shared the knowledge of why anyone would buy such ugly apparel. Then he laughed, glanced at his own glove and rolled his eyes. We needed no language. We were brothers united by a common need to save our fingers and to heck with fashion sense and decorum. I chuckled about that look he gave me for most of the day. I still laugh now!

If that was my highlight, my low point was at the end of the day. I was stupid. Really stupid. The day was one of climbs and descents. I had an issue with my sock about midday and changed it in Melide. And yeah, yet again no one batted an eye as I changed my socks in the street. Anyhow, I put a dollop of Vaseline on my toes, donned fresh socks and set off. The rest of the afternoon was fine until about 5k from Arzúa. My right foot started to hurt. The little toe was feeling a bit raw. I checked my phone. An hour to go. It would be fine. With 1k to go I was definitely limping to compensate for the pain and to keep as much weight off my right side. Why didn't I stop? Why didn't I do what I would have told anyone else to do? Stop, sort it out, make it good and go again. I don't know. It was cold? I was nearly there? I was stupid? Yeah, the last one. Definitely.

I arrived into Arzúa at about 4:30pm and, head down concentrating on my phone map, I found my digs, a fantastic apartment called Berce. Well equipped, beautifully appointed. The bathroom was huge and had a bath. I remember thinking, 'Um, I wonder if the Camino is providing that because I'm going to need it.' Sitting down I took my right boot off, and my right sock and the top of my 'right' little toe. Part of the sock stayed attached to my foot.

A half hour later, soaking in the warm water of the bath, I had managed to separate sock from skin, but much like in *Jaws* when Chief Brody says, "You're going to need a bigger boat," my small blister plasters were not going to come close to fixing my toe and the wound dressings I had in my first aid kit also weren't suitable. I needed a pharmacy with a knowledgeable pharmacist who spoke English well enough so that I didn't have to rely on my Spanish. This wasn't getting a couple of holes in a boot mended. I'd walked into town from the east. My foot had been sore and I had concentrated on finding my accommodation. I pulled up my phone map and searched for *Farmacia*. The nearest result was about a 10-minute walk away. Piece of cake, usually.

Strapping my foot as best I could, I donned clean socks and gingerly pulled my boots on. Trying to hike around town with a sandal strap cutting across my toes was not a wise idea. I took a breath and determined to go find a chemist. Walking out of No. 37 Rúa Padre Pardo, I stopped quite suddenly. There, opposite me, at No. 34 Rúa Padre Pardo, was a pharmacy. Five steps away.

The pharmacist spoke fluent English and invited me to remove my boot and sock. She got me wipes to clean it, a perfect ointment to sanitise it, and a dressing to pad and protect it. She also supplied me with enough of everything to last me about a week.

"Probably fine in a few days once you finish the Camino. How does it feel?"

I flexed my toe inside my boot, "It feels fine. No problems at all. Thank you."

"My pleasure. Lucky you were close by, yes?"

I thanked her, paid and left. As I was walking into town for a dinner with P² and Mark, I met up again with Andrea and Blanca. They'd had a good day, if cold. They enquired after mine. I told them I'd hurt my toe, but the Camino had provided an expert opposite my accommodation. Such was the shared experience of how that type of thing seems to happen, they merely nodded and said, "Yes. That seems to be how it works."

After a dinner in the main square that is best not written about, (I'll merely say it was dire) we called it a night. We have two days to go. Tomorrow is going to be chilly and raining. Planned distance: 19km from here to O Pedrouzo. I mean, with that total of kilometres, it is practically a rest day!

Steps walked: 41,028
Camino distance travelled: 29.94kms
Total elevation ascents: 664m
Total descents: 822m

Day 25

April 30th 2024
Arzúa – O Pedrouzo
Planned distance: 19kms

As you are now used to, at the end of each day I put the total steps and total distance. Well today, I also know that the total rainfall was 9mm, which sounds like a mere drip in a puddle. It isn't. It is a lot. It is a soaked to the skin amount. When we all stopped for a much-needed warm drink around lunchtime, a rare glimpse of the sun caused us to steam gently, like a pan of simmering pilgrims.

Most of the day was full of heavy clouds, light to medium to heavy rain, but mercifully no wind. A straight-down-downpour that far from making me sad, made me joyous. I had a poncho, water-proof boots and all things considered, it is only water. It did limit photo opportunities, but there is something grounding, humbling and almost spiritual about walking in the rain. There's nothing you can do; no control you can exert to stop it and so you simply smile and keep going. Be happy. Greet your fellow walkers in a positive way.

Ah, but a lot of the replies were mere grunts. It seemed some of those tramping through the wet were less than happy. Some, who started in Sarria on Saturday, have had a challenging few days. Snow, overcast skies, little sun and a lot of rain and mud. They've seen nothing of the conditions Paddy, Popper and I had in our first few weeks and so I somehow felt I had to be even more positive for them.

Halfway through the morning I met a fellow happy walker. I'll come to her in a moment or two, but she arrived alongside me after

I had been thinking about the whys and wherefores of doing the Camino. Over the last few days, Mark and Paddy have been popping in and out of various churches along the Way. I tend to ask, flippantly, that if they are saying a prayer inside, then say one for me... I mean, it can't hurt... can it? Yet, on the occasions when the topic of 'The Church' has come up more seriously, they know that I want nothing to do with established religions. In what some may consider harsh language; I detest the organisations made by men that purport to be godly. Especially that which I have been closest to; the religion that surrounded me since birth. Given I was raised within a certain sect of Christianity, I feel I can express views on it, but don't get me wrong, if you wholeheartedly believe in a faith and the structures that surround it, I have no issues with you. My issues are my own.

Also, don't get me wrong on the whole belief thing... I totally believe that Jesus was a real person, a provable historical figure who was likely to have been a radically rebellious, amazingly kind-hearted and charismatic leader. I think his socialist ideas and anger at the money being made in the temples were probably what singled him out for persecution. He even features quite heavily in my first book, an alternative history novel with a religious twist. As I was researching background information for the plot, I became sure from the type of followers he gathered, that Jesus believed in the equality of men and women, Jew and gentile, Judeans and Romans.

I definitely believe that a lot of what he taught was corrupted after his execution and that any 'Divine Doctrine' was invented by shallow men occupying gaudy palaces. But do I think the central tenet of Christianity (and every other religion that exists), namely, *'do unto others what you would have them do to you'* is a good idea? Of course I do.

My primary concern is that whilst I think Jesus thought and taught the same, nowhere did he mention a caveat of 'Unless'. You know... treat each person as you wish to be treated, *unless* they are a different nationality, colour, creed, gender, sexual orientation or any other thing you don't like. That seems to be what a lot of the more zealous types in the world today are preaching. I am mistrustful of the Unless crowd.

Anyway, thoughts such as these had occasionally surfaced during my Camino, but it is a pilgrimage, so that's okay. Yet they were not occupying much of my time. I wasn't doing this for any spiritual re-awakening or religious epiphany. I could look at the inside of churches and cathedrals and be awed by the crafts and labour that went into them, but my spirituality was not the reason I was walking. Wanting to walk the Camino, doing it to prove I still could and doing it with old friends were my reasons. God would have been a long way down any list I had to draw up.

Yet, on this wet and bedraggled 30th of April, which, in eastern Christianity, is the feast day of St James (yep, the same disciple James that is buried in Santiago… allegedly) I did ponder for a moment or two about the motivations of others on the road. Were they doing this for 'proper' pilgrim's reasons or like me were they just out for a long walk, but like I said, I wasn't pondering for too long. Just passing thoughts on a rainy, introspective sort of a day. And then, a couple of hours into the morning I said a happy, "Buen Camino" to a fellow walker and instead of the grunt I had been receiving from most of the newbie walkers that day, I got a beaming smile and a cheery, "Buen Camino" in return. We fell into step alongside each other.

Jess is an Anglian priest from England. She, like me, was soaked by this stage of the day and happily resigned to it.

We spoke at length of the Camino, the changing nature of it (the increased commercialism and numbers of walkers) since Sarria. We shared our observations of our fellow walkers. The newbies from Sarria who were wet and miserable, and the 'oldies' from further back along the Way who were wet and buoyant.

Jess had started at StJPdP in mid-March and will finish, like me, in Santiago tomorrow. Her older sister and their mother will meet and celebrate Jess's achievement the following day, on Thursday the

2nd of May. It wasn't planned to happen on that day and yet, when Jess realised what date it would occur on she was both surprised and accepting. The date will mark the second anniversary of her Father's passing. His name was Douglas and she is sure he has walked every step of the Way with her.

Is that an intimate detail to share with someone you met an hour or so earlier on a rainy roadway? Yeah, I would say it was… normally. But not on the Camino. On here, it was the most natural thing in the world. On here, you and your fellow pilgrims connect at a different level. Is that spiritual? Perhaps.

After our 'steaming' lunch stop, when Jess and I caught up to, or were caught up by, Paddy, Popper and Mark, we set off again into a grey drizzle of serenity.

Jess and I continued to talk… of faith, established religions, my dislike of them, her path into her Church, colleagues who are easy to work with and those that aren't. We spoke of how priests and bishops were as guilty of shortcomings as those secular types I had worked with in my career(s). We shared stories of people being heard and acknowledged and people being ignored in their times of real need. I told her of the 'shorthand' that my wife had told me about. For those who really need someone to listen to them, but whose request might get lost in the daily noise, all they need do is message, 'I need 8 minutes of your time.' It's a request that means, 'Now. Please. I need to talk.' We agreed it's a genius idea.

Eventually we had talked so much that, after walking through an almost Australian-esque collection of eucalyptus gum trees, we walked into O Pedrouzo; our 'short' day completed. We said farewell and I sought out my digs. A shower, a change of clothes and then I went in search of a laundrette. There was one ten yards away and so all of today's clothes got washed and, more importantly, dried. A short break and then dinner with my three amigos.

We sat with Italians, a Canadian called Paul, Hannah from Dublin (whom we first met almost a week ago in Villafranca) and a lady called Aleksandra, who now lives in Wisconsin. She started in Burgos and for a large part of her journey she has walked with a fellow woman 'pilgrim' she met on the road. The two women are not unusual in meeting and walking together, but Aleksandra is originally from Russia and her travelling companion is Ukrainian. They have walked in friendship and mutual respect, reflecting on the tragedy that is unfolding because of misguided leaders and ambitious men and how, were more people to walk the Camino with their supposed adversaries, perhaps the world would be kinder. I think they might be right.

As I returned to my bed for the night, I figured that for someone who hadn't intended to ponder the nature of spirituality, religion and the applicability of a 'pilgrimage' in the modern world, I hadn't done too bad today. I could tick that off my list.

Tomorrow is our final day on the Camino Francés. Twenty kilometres left. A couple more hills, a bit more rain and a large cathedral as our goal. The supposed resting place of Saint James, or in Spanish, Sant Iago. He was, according to scripture, a cousin of Jesus, (his mother was Salome, sister to Mary). He was a bit bad tempered and fiery, one of the first to join the Apostles, the second to die (after Judas Iscariot), and the first to be martyred. His father was Zebedee. And now, with this huge day ahead, I am somehow reminded, it's time for bed.

P.S. Anne and Graeme, if you are reading this, Jess was intrigued about Two Steps Forward, so she bought the e-book!!

Steps walked: 32,147
Camino distance travelled: 20.83kms
Total elevation ascents: 474m
Total descents: 573m
Total rainfall: 9mm

Day 26

May 1st 2024
O Pedrouzo – Santiago de Compostela
Planned distance: 21kms

Here it is. The last day of our Camino. A strange day of hellos, farewells, bizarre coincidences and accidental meetings, all of it set to the rhythm of the kilometre markers we have been so used to for the last four weeks. Yet today, rather than feeling grateful as each kilometre dropped off the total, (meaning we were closer to the end of our day and a warm shower, meal and bed) I felt a poignant mix of gratitude, that my friends and I had been able to do such a journey, and of course, a tinge of sadness that the 'adventure' was coming to its end.

We would later find out that a total of 1,989 pilgrims registered their arrival in Santiago on the 1st of May 2024. But we know that the figure was missing at least one, (Paddy) as he decided to go into the office on the following morning. Conservatively then, probably 2,000 people entered a city of almost 100,000. The pilgrims on the Francés Way left from various starting points at different times and still, in the first kilometre of today, there was Pierre, our 77-year-young Swiss friend.

As we exited O Pedrouzo, through a ground mist topped with blue skies which made the landscape look like the veils of time were parting, a majestic tree towered over the landscape. I stopped to take a photograph. Behind me, Pierre said, "Hello, Ian."

This was his last day on a journey that's been six years in the making. I had wanted to wish him well since we'd briefly passed on the road to Arzúa on day 24, and now, wish granted, here he was. We embraced and bade each other a fond farewell and a Buen Camino. He'd be walking, as he always did, at his own pace.

Later, when the sun had burnt off the mist, and the skies revealed occasional scudding rain clouds, we met David and Ivan again, also the Italians from last night and Hannah and Paul. The ends were being tidied up, goodbyes and best wishes being exchanged.

Our little band of four 'Larne boys' had decided that should we become spread out as usual, then five kilometres or so from the outskirts of Santiago we would stop, regroup and walk in together. That said, we also noticed that in these last stages, a lot of the kilometre markers had been defaced.

There were differing accounts on this from later conversations. Some Spanish thought that the 'short-distance' pilgrims doing Sarria to Santiago, were taking them as souvenirs. Some thought it was the locals as a protest at the ever-increasing numbers of pilgrims coming through their quiet villages and towns. This latter theory seemed to gain credence as nearing Santiago, we noticed graffiti sprayed signs and in one place, actual printed signs, with anti-Camino sentiments.

I don't know the truth and my Spanish wasn't good enough to get the nuances of either the signs or the conversations. Yet this was a month or two before more stringent protests against tourism took place in the likes of Barcelona.

However, the lack of reliable markers meant we couldn't risk meeting at a particular one, so we identified a café attached to the San Marcos Camping Grounds and suggested it as a rendezvous. That is why we stopped in a little café, that if we hadn't suggested it, I'd have probably walked on by.

I arrived along with Paddy. We were joined by Mark and Popper a few minutes later. After grabbing a table, I waited at the counter to be served, casually looking around the narrow space. Sitting on her own, with her back to me, was Belen from Madrid, who I had met first on day 19 when she and Tessa had been in the restaurant run by Dianna and Adrian. She almost cried when I said, "Hi." It wasn't the reaction I'd been expecting! Turns out she'd been walking mostly on her own since I'd last seen her in the café in O Cebreiro, but a few days ago, she'd hurt her leg. Struggling through the pain, she had reached San Marcos and was on the verge of giving up. She didn't think she could walk the last 5km and all the pilgrims passing by were strangers. About to call a taxi, she instead asked if she could walk with us. Of course!

I cheered her up a bit by telling her that I had walked with Tessa a few days ago. She wished she'd had the chance to say goodbye to the young American. After some food and drink, our new, bigger band, set out on the final trek.

About an hour later, somewhat drenched, but with beaming smiles across our five faces, we entered the last 100 metres amidst a huge gathering of joyful 'workers'. The 1st of May is Labour Day, a public holiday in Spain. Yet, in the midst of a wild throng of people, there was Colin's wife, Michelle, waiting in exactly the right place to greet us. Just as well too, for actually finding the cathedral in Santiago once you are cloistered in the narrow streets, is a task in itself. All those amazing signs that we'd followed since France seem to stop in the middle of the town. I guess they reckon any fool could find the cathedral at that stage. Well, perhaps, but not us, so thank goodness for Michelle.

The six of us walked round the corner and into the square in front of the cathedral. As we took photos of our arrival, in the midst of a heaving throng of humanity, Tessa was suddenly there, joyous and laughing at being reunited with her buddy, Belen. Next to her was Andrea and her mum Blanca who had walked alongside Diana and her son Derrick. I found it both surreal and completely under-standable that in the midst of thousands of people, here were our 'Camino friends'. Even when Mark and I went to register our arrival, (number 1020 and 1021 of the day) the person behind us in the queue was Aleksandra, the Russian lady from the restaurant last night.

And then it was done. Our Camino complete. The company of many lost to the swirling masses. Mark and I visited the imposing cathedral to see the place where the relics of St James are meant to be held. The small silver reliquary that has drawn millions of pilgrims over a thousand years or more. Even then, someone was looking out for these two lads from Craigyhill, for as we entered the cathedral there was no one in front of us.

One small aside here. You cannot enter through the main doors that you see in the movie 'The Way' nor can you place your hand on the spot that apparently pilgrims have touched in gratitude throughout history. Nope. The main door is only for Spanish Royalty apparently. Nor were we lucky enough to see the massive incense burner, the Botafumeiro, swinging. That is reserved for special days usually, but in November 2023 a screw from the support mechanism landed on the altar during a mass. It was decided to take the whole thing down and give it a thorough service. Fair enough. It is big and you don't want it falling on you. Apparently it has fallen a few times, including infamously when Catherine of Aragon visited on her way to marry Prince Arthur. While it was being swung, the Botafumeiro flew out of the cathedral through the Platerias high window. No one was injured, but if you were looking for an omen, it's a shame the young Princess Catherine didn't pick up on it. Arthur married her, then died and she became Henry VIII's first wife.

Anyway, using the side door entrance and not seeing a swinging incense burner didn't detract from the fact that Mark and I seemed to have the place to ourselves. There were a few people in the pews, but no queues like I had expected. We walked unhindered into the crypt, the reputed burial place of Saint James the Great, the apostle of Jesus Christ. No one hurried us, no one was to our front or back. We stood there contemplating until we decided to make our way out. As we exited up and behind the nave, we could hear a rising babble of voices. By the time we had come round again to the entrance to the crypt there was a queue almost out the door of the cathedral. Good timing!

Also good timing, or so I thought, was when we exited from the Pilgrim's Office after getting our Compostelas. Mark and I were greeted by… well, I am not sure how to sensitively describe the young lady that greeted us. Charming, charismatic and engaging yes, but more simply put, she was beautiful. Wearing faded blue jeans and a plain t-shirt, she smiled beguilingly and asked, in a home-counties accent, if we spoke English.

"Yes."

"Oh good. There are some meeting rooms upstairs, split up by language groups. You can go up; we have tea and biscuits if you would like?"

"We?"

"We're a volunteer group who look out for pilgrims."

I think that's what she said… She could have said, "We are a biker gang looking for recruits," for in truth, I wasn't paying that much attention to her words and I mean, who isn't going to take up the offer of free tea and biscuits. Or should that be… who isn't, if not two older eejits that should know better, and who should definitely realise that nothing in life is free. But the young lady was hard to refuse and so Mark and I wandered up to the room. Sure enough, tea and biscuits were provided by a couple of older women, dressed in modestly long robed skirts and t-shirts with a logo that I couldn't quite make out.

We were joined over the next few minutes by about ten other English-speaking pilgrims. We had tea. And biscuits. By the time we were encouraged to take a seat, in what I definitely recognised as a circle of chairs, I was in no doubt about what had happened. Another older lady entered, we'll call her Louise, dressed in a modern version of a distinctive uniform. As we chatted, I learnt that the Faithful Companions of Jesus was founded in Amiens in France in 1820 by Marie Madeleine de Bonnault d'Hoüet. Nowadays, under their

Camino Companions project in Santiago de Compostela, they offer pilgrims a space to articulate and find meaning at the end of their Camino. Personally, as the group quietened down and centred, I couldn't help thinking that 'Hot Nun' had been used as an effective lure. Mark summed it up later, better than I could.

"I don't think they'd get as many taking up the offer of free tea and biscuits if they sent Sister Louise downstairs."

As it was, weirdly, I kinda liked reflecting on their first question. Why did you come on the Camino?

"To walk with friends, to reminisce on how far we have come in life and to look forward to what we will do next. To make a memory and to have an adventure."

Alas, when they got to the second question about God and His meaning to us as pilgrims, I had to politely decline.

"I am sorry, Sister. I do respect you and your fellow Sisters, and I understand the value of what you offer to those of faith, but I have a hard time with the church you are part of, so I shall say thank you for the tea and biscuits and take my leave."

Sister Louise and her companions wished we well and offered me the blessings of God. It would have been churlish not to accept them. I had, after all, taken their biscuits.

***

After retrieving the package Paddy and I had sent on from Pamplona, (fast efficient service in the post office about ten steps away from the hotel) and the luggage that I had sent from Saint-Jean-Pied-de-Port (fast efficient recovery from the store in a hostel about 6k away from the hotel, for which I took a cab), we five, Colin, Michelle, Mark, Paddy and myself went to, Udon, a Japanese restaurant for dinner. Well, where else would you eat in Spain? The food was amazing (best meal I have had in a long time) and the craic, mighty. We laughed and reminisced and at no point did we discuss what time we had to get up, or the distance we would be walking or the likely weather. It felt like a first step back into the real world.

At the end of the night, we wandered back through the narrow-cobbled streets of Santiago, to the Hotel Rua Villar. One of the 'treat' hotels we had booked for the trip. And it was. Within a few steps of the cathedral, it is an eighteenth-century manor house that was converted into a family-run hotel in 2004. Also, with a bit of expense comes exceptional service. Yes, the receptionist could book me a taxi to take me to the airport when I needed it. Yes, there were some decent shoe shops in the 'new' town. Yes, we can take any clothes you might not want and donate them to charity.

All of which meant that the following day I could offload the Camino emblazoned heavy jumper and the ugliest pair of gloves I have ever owned. Yet, like the rest of the last month, I hoped I'd not forget them.

Steps walked: 34,922
Camino distance travelled: 21.23kms
Total elevation ascents: 434m
Total descents: 475m

THE AFTERWARDS

Day Plus 1 and 2 and now…

2nd May 2024
Santiago de Compostela
Planned distance: None
Planned steps: However many I need.

After a relaxed breakfast, I took some time out to thoroughly clean my trekking poles and replace their rubber feet with shiny new ones (and yes, I had carried a couple of spare sets so that I could do this at the end). It might not seem a big deal, but given our quarantine laws, trying to get anything back into Australia is a task and a half. Making sure my trekking poles were pristine and with no traces of soil or vegetation on them was vital. Alas, my poor old boots would not be so easy.

What with preliminary training and the Camino, they had done 1500kms. They had three stitches (in time) applied to the sides in Santo Domingo de la Calzada and in the last week, had been snowed on, soaked, mud-laden, farm-'mud'-laden and then dried to a crisp 'brownish' hue. There was no way they'd get back into Australia short of being steam-cleaned, and I'd inconveniently left my industrial boot steam-cleaner elsewhere. Solution: new boots. Fortuitously, there is a brand of Spanish boots, 'Panama Jacks', that I am partial to, and so, armed with the receptionist's recommendations, I set off in the mid-morning drizzle to get myself a pair of 'Panamas'. I even managed to get by in Spanish enough to ask the kind shop attendants if there was a local charity I could donate my old boots to. One of the ladies said she would take them to her church where they would be cleaned and given a new, deserving home. Job done. I thanked them and then, before handing the boots over, I took a farewell picture. I imagine the ladies in the shop thought I was *un poco loco*.

The five of us met up for a final dinner together, and a few drinks. Then I was set for an early night. My flight was at 'silly-o'clock' in the morning.

Total steps for today: 14,758. Total distance: no idea. Probably about 10k wandering around Santiago but I don't think it counts.

The following morning, at 4:30am, I was up and out, catching a flight from Santiago to Madrid, and from Madrid to the UK so I could attend a book fair. I decided I would draw a line under my step count when I got to the bar in St Ives Cambridgeshire, where I'd be meeting my fellow organisers of the book fair. I couldn't have planned it much better, for literally as I walked into that bar and got a beer, the step counter on my watch registered the 5,140th step of the day. It brought my final totals to:

- Total Steps since arriving in Perth airport, 1,000,001

- Total distance walked on the Camino Francés (measuring point to point locations): 556.26kms (and 244kms by train)

- Highest Point: 1,509m

- Total Ascents: 15,428m

- Total Descents: 15,218

- (And just for me) my weight on 1st of May, 72.2kgs

Nationalities I spoke to on the Way:
American, Argentinian, Australian, Belgian, Brazilian, Canadian, Chinese, Columbian, Czech, Danish, Dutch, English, Finish, French, German, Irish (Northern and Southern), Israeli, Italian, Japanese, Luxembourgian, Mexican, New Zealander, Norwegian, Portuguese,

Russian, Scottish, South African, South Korean, Spanish, Taiwanese, Ukrainian, Venezuelan, Welsh, and one New Caledonian.

And that was my Camino story.

The Camino Francés from Saint-Jean-Pied-de-Port to Santiago de Compostella. A total distance of some 800kms that we walked over 550kms of and took a train for the remainder.

Would I do it again? Maybe not all of it, but only because I've done it already. Yet, as I am typing this, my tickets to Spain are already booked. From the 16th to the 26th of April 2025, I will be walking those pesky 244kms from Burgos to Astorga. This time I will be on my own, but not really, as I have confidence that each and every day I will meet pilgrims whose stories and life experiences will keep me fuelled up for the journey ahead. That seems to *my* way of doing *the* Way. I also think that on this ancient road, you'll never walk alone. For even in solitude, the Camino is looking out for you.

Buen Camino!

Bye boots, and thanks!

Acknowledgements

To Popper first and foremost, thank you for messaging me, "Hey Ian. Here's a thought..." It was a great idea mate, and it wouldn't have happened without you.

Also, of course, Paddy, Mark, Michael and Gerry. It wouldn't have been the same (or half as funny) without your input to it all. (I shall also include here, Paddy's thanks to the *mantequilla* and strawberry jam manufactures of Europe).

To Jacki, thanks for saying no to the idea back in 2018 and for saying yes to the idea in 2023. I know you didn't 'give me permission' but it would have been a lot more difficult without your cooperation.

Thanks also to Anne and Graham for inspiring me in the first place, to Seana for *preparándome para hablar español*, and to all those I met along the Way, whether mentioned in here or not, for keeping me inspired on the journey.

Thanks also to the hosts, the waiting staff, the restaurateurs, café owners and of course, bar staff, who kept us going. A special shout out to the pharmacists who 'sponsored' a couple of days...

And finally, to the plumbers of Spain. I am humbled and grateful.

About the Author

Ian Hooper grew up in the coastal town of Larne, Northern Ireland. He joined the Royal Air Force at age eighteen and worked initially as an aircraft technician before being commissioned as an Intelligence Officer. After serving for two decades, he and his Australian wife relocated to the southwest of Western Australia.

In 2014, writing under the pen name of Ian Andrew, his first novel, *A Time to Every Purpose*, was released to critical acclaim, and in 2018, the first of his 'Wright and Tran' crime series, *Face Value,* won the Publishers Weekly Booklife prize for fiction.

He is now the executive director of independent publisher, Leschenault Press and its imprint, The Book Reality Experience, as well as being an author, editor and ghost-writer. In addition, he is the co-founder of the international series of independent author book fairs. A fellow of the Australian Institute of Management, he holds qualifications in management, training, and learning design as well as a master's in creative writing.

Living in rural Western Australia, surrounded by a resident mob of kangaroos, he is currently working on the next novel in the Wright & Tran series of detective stories.

RESOURCES

Kit List

I said at the start of this book, I wouldn't be dolling out advice, as my goodness there are a lot of folks doing that about the Camino… especially when it comes to kit lists. I truly believe in, 'take what you want'. If it's too heavy, ditch it or send it on to Santiago, or better still, use the daily donkey services to send it forward day by day. Yet I realise some will want to know what I took. So, after a lot of contemplation as to whether I should include it or not, here is my kit list.

Oh, and if I was forced to give advice, it would be to prepare by buying your kit in good time and testing it. If it works for you, then great. Also, know how it works. That always helps.

I took some things that I sent forward to Santiago and shouldn't have. Even though I didn't see them for most of the Camino, I will list them here, because I should have kept them and ended up buying replacements when I couldn't feel my fingers in O Pedrouzo.

Walking equipment and 'gadgets'

1 x **Osprey®** ATMOS AG 65L back pack (from Cotswold Outdoors, UK, who get a mention for their generous veterans' discount)

2 x **Spanker™** Elite Bottle Carriers – to carry bottles of water, sports electrolyte drinks, or:

2 x **Osprey** 500ml hydraulics soft flasks. They allowed me to top up and monitor my water far easier than an in-pack bladder

2 x carabiners and a couple of plastic clothes pegs to clip things on to 'me' (hat, gloves etc) without having to remove the pack

1x set of **Mountain Designs™** Tread Cork Trekking Poles

1 x mini-first aid kit (17cm by 13cm by 5cm thick) comprising:

   2 x compression bandages

   1 x triangular bandage

   1 x emergency insulation silver rescue sheet

   1 x medium wound dressing, 1 x large wound dressing

   8 x compeed™ toe blister plasters, 4 x compeed medium blister plasters, 2 x compeed large blister plasters

   Pack of safety pins

   20 x antiseptic wipes

   Surgical tape, Prima tape

   1 x large tub of Vaseline™ (for toes and feet)

   Painkillers, Anti-inflammatory tablets, Imodium and other meds

1 x **Scruba™** Wash Bag (for in room laundry)
1 x **Scruba** pegless clothesline
40 x **re-stor**® laundry sheets

1 x 'Waiter' corkscrew (knife, corkscrew, bottle opener)

1 x stainless steel collapsible cup, (I'd take a silicone one next time)

1 x pen torch, with 2 x AA batteries. Used it once on the whole trip. Next time I will take a small square one that clips to my backpack and lasts over a month on a single USB charge.

1 x Bone Conduction Headphones. Fourth best gadget I had on the Camino. Honestly, I used them more before and after than I did on the walk, but they are superb and do not cut you off from your surroundings. One charge lasted all day.

1 x **Nitecore™** NB10000 GEN2 Ultra-Slim Power Bank, 10000mAh – Third best gadget I had. It is an ultra-light powerbank capable of charging an iPhone three times over.

1 x **Disgian™** Travel Adapter, Universal International Power Adapter with 3xUSB Ports and Type-C. Second best gadget. A multi-national adaptor with built in USB ports. I plugged it in each night and it did my headphones, my phone, my power bank and my...

1 x **Garmin™** Forerunner345 Music Watch – THE best bit of kit I had on the Camino. My wife bought it for me and I initially thought it was a bit of overkill, but I loved it. Accurate, good charge retention and (once you figure it out) easy to use. Absolutely fantastic. Even now, a year later, I can look up the stats of each day I walked on the Camino.

Clothes

1 x **Columbia**® Men's Crestwood Waterproof Mid Hiking Boots Cordovan Squash
1 x **Teva**® Original Universal sandals (to wear in the evenings)
1 x pair of Fluid® fingerless trekking gloves
1 x large blue ALTUS® Atmospheric poncho
1 x hat (with wide brim for sun protection)
1 x sunglasses
1 x **Buff**® neck wrap
1 x fleece
3 x **RAB** tee-shirts (one long sleeve, 2 x short)
2 x **Geared** ultra-lightweight shorts
3 x **NuYarn** Ergonomic Hiking Socks by **Kathmandu**®
3 x underwear
Not strictly clothes, but 1 x silk (permethrin treated) sleeping bag liner

Things I had but sent ahead instead of keeping with me:
    1 x wool beanie
    1 x merino lightweight insulation jumper
    1 x pair cold weather gloves
    1 x lightweight full length trekking trousers

Wash kit

Strictly speaking I probably only needed a toothbrush and deodorant, as most of the accommodations supplied everything else, but I didn't know that for sure and so I took:

1 x small bar soap
1 x small bar shampoo
1 x disposable razor
1 x roll-on deodorant
1 x toothbrush
1 x travel toothpaste
1 x hairbrush
1 x small container of face cream
2 x small tubes of sunscreen
1 x pair of nail scissors (more important than you'd think – keep your toenails trimmed)
1 x lipbalm (again, more important than you'd think. The sun and wind will definitely attack your lips)
1 x large microfibre towel

These next three items I carried easily accessible on all days. As I mentioned, most places you stop at have a toilet. Most do **not** have paper, soap or towels.

> 1 x mini microfibre towel (and by mini I mean tiny)
> 1 x packet of Sea-to-Summit™ soap wavers
> Some toilet roll

And that was it. **Total weight: 7.5kg.**

I did have the Osprey Airporter for protecting my backpack and trekking poles on the long-haul flight from Oz, but I didn't carry this with me and sent it on to Santiago. I intend to do the same (and send it on to Astorga) next time around as it does weigh quite a bit, is bulky and I won't need it on the walk.

Accommodation List

All my accommodation was at least good to very good, bar the one in Palais de Rei and even it wasn't that bad. However, I will highlight those that were standouts.

Citadines Montparnasse Paris
67 Avenue Du Maine, 14th arr., Paris, 75014, France

Hotel Itzalpea
5 place du Trinquet, Saint-Jean-Pied-de Port, Saint-Jean-Pied-de-Port, France 64220

Well worth the extra money after the Pyrenees and a great hotel.
Hotel Roncesvalles
Mayor, s/n, Roncesvalles, 31650, Spain

Casa Batit
San Pedro 18B, Viscarret-Guerendiáin, 31695, Spain

Txantxorena
Calle la Zatoya, 5, Zubiri, Navarra, 31630, ES

Pamplonapartments Pozo Blanco
20 Calle del Pozo Blanco, Pamplona, 31001, Spain

Hotel El Cerco
Rodrigo Ximenez de Rada, 36, Puente la Reina, 31100, Spain

Apartamento medieval en el Camino De Santiago
Calle Rua Kalea,19, Estella, 31200, Spain

Hostal Suetxe
Carramendavia s/n, Los Arcos, 31210, Spain

The first rest day and therefore a more luxurious hotel:
Hotel Gran Via
Avda Gran Vía Rey Juan Carlos I 71 Bis, Logroño, Logroño, Spain,
26005 Logroño, Logroño, España

Apartamentos Vino y Camino
C/ Arrabal de la Estrella, 46, Nájera, 26300, Spain

Hotel - Hostel Atuvera
Calle Mayor N.º 6 - 8, Santo Domingo de la Calzada, 26250, Spain

Caminante
Calle Mayor, 36, 09250 Belorado, Spain

SANSIL Atapuerca
Calle San Vicente nº 7, Atapuerca, 09199, Spain

Excellent
Bella Vista Catedral-Apartamentos
Calle Fernán González 40 3 C, Burgos, 09003, Spain

Napoleon's former digs
Posada Real Casa de Tepa
Santiago, 2, Astorga, Astorga, Spain 24700

Great little place
El Trasgu de Foncebadón
Real s/n, Foncebadón, 24722, Spain

Hostal Virgen de la Encina
Gil y Carrasco, 3, Ponferrada, 24401, Spain

Viña Femita
Avenida Calvo Sotelo 2, Villafranca del Bierzo, 24500, Spain

Habitaciones Frade
O cebreiro, O Cebreiro, 27671, Spain

Complexo Xacobeo
C/ Leoncio Cadorniga Carro, Tríacastela, 27630, Spain

Albareda piso super-céntrico en Sarria
52 Rua Calvo Sotelo, Sarria, 27600, Spain

My favourite
Alojamientos con encanto Ruliña
Portomarin, 27170, Spain

Pensión Restaurante Casa Camiño II
Travesia del Peregrino No 8, Palas de Rei, 27200, Spain

Excellent
Berce
39 Rúa Padre Pardo 5ºB, Arzúa, 15810, Spain

PR Una Estrella Dorada
Avenida De Lugo n 10-1, O Pedrouzo, 15821, Spain

Excellent, and the perfect way to end
Hotel Rua Villar
Rúa do Vilar, 8 - 10, Santiago De Compostela Old Town, Santiago
De Compostela, Spain, 15705

Apps

All Trails: AllTrails is a mobile app and website that helps users find and plan outdoor activities like hiking, biking, and running, offering detailed trail maps, reviews, and photos from the community.

Buen Camino: Buen Camino is a guide app for pilgrims doing the Way of St James on foot or by bike, published by Editorial Buen Camino SL. For any questions or comments about the App, contact: info@editorialbuencamino.com
or visit: www.editorialbuencamino.com

Tripit: TripIt is an award-winning travel organizing app that keeps all your details in one place.

Youtube Channels

Type in Camino in the search bar and you will be inundated, but the ones I watched the most were:
https://www.youtube.com/@robscamino
https://www.youtube.com/@backpackingJas
https://www.youtube.com/@SamandKelly
https://www.youtube.com/@lostamonglocals5382

And for learning Basque – check this channel out:
https://www.youtube.com/@HellaBasque

Printed in Great Britain
by Amazon

61696943R00137